Story, Song, and Law: The Craft of Preaching in Today's Church

STORY, SONG, AND LAW: THE CRAFT OF PREACHING IN TODAY'S CHURCH

David Brindley

BRITISH AND FOREIGN BIBLE SOCIETY
Stonehill Green, Westlea, Swindon, SN5 7DG, England

A catalogue record for this book is available from the British Library
ISBN 0564 088757

Typeset by BFBS Production Services Department (TP Section)
Printed in Great Britain by Biddles Ltd, Guildford
Cover design by Litchfield Morris, Gloucester

Bible Societies exist to provide resources for Bible distribution and use. The British and Foreign Bible Society (BFBS) is a member of the United Bible Societies, an international partnership working in over 180 countries. Their common aim is to reach all people with the Bible, or some part of it, in a language they can understand and at a price they can afford. Parts of the Bible have now been translated into over 2,000 languages. Bible Societies aim to help every church at every point where it uses the Bible. You are invited to share in this work by your prayers and gifts. The Bible Society in your country will be very happy to provide details of its activity.

DEEP in the shadows of the past,
  Far out from settled lands,
Some nomads travelled with their God
  Across the desert sands.
The dawn of hope for humankind
  Was glimpsed by them alone—
A promise calling them ahead,
  A future yet unknown.

While others bowed to changeless gods,
  They me a mystery:
God with umcompleted name,
  'I am what I will be';
And by their tents, around their fires,
  In *story, song and law*,
They praised, remembered, handed on
  A past that promised more.

From Abraham to Nazareth
The promise changed and grew,
  While some, remembering the past,
Recorded what they knew,
  And some, in letters or laments,
In prophecy and praise,
  Recovered held and re-expressed
New Hope for changing days.

For all the writing that survived,
  For leaders, long ago,
The sifted, chose, and then preserved
  The Bible that we know,
Give thanks, and find its promise yet
  Our comfort, strength, and call,
The working model for our faith,
  Alive with hope for all.

Brian A. Wren (1936–)

ACKNOWLEDGEMENTS

The publisher would like to thank the following for permission to reproduce copyright material in this book.

Church House Publishing for extracts from the report *Good News in our Times* © Central Broad of Finance of the Church of England;

Georgia Weidenfield & Nicholson for extracts from the *Persistence of Faith* by Jonathan Sacks © Weidenfield & Nicholson;

Mowbrays for extracts from *Preaching from the Old Testament* by D. W. Cleverly Ford;

SCM Press Ltd for extracts from *Homiletics* by David Butterick © SCM Press Ltd 1987;

the Society for the Promotion of Christian Knowledge for extracts from *Speaking of God* by Trevor Dennis and *The Sermon Slot* by Sharon Swaine;

Methodist Publishing House for extracts from *Faith & Worship* © Local Preachers' Training Course;

Virgin Books for extracts from *Your Voice and How to Use it Successfully* by Cecily Berry © Virgin Publishing House;

Hodder & Stoughton for extracts from *I believe in Preaching* by John Slott ©Hodder & Stoughton.

We have made every effort to contact copyright holders, and apologize if we have inadvertently overlooked anyone's copyright. Any oversights will be corrected in a subsequent reprint of the book.

CONTENTS

PREFACE

For the last ten years I have been teaching a large number of ministers and students for ministry to preach. In particular, the students of the West of England Ministerial Training Course have worked with much of the material in this book. In the light of their comments and reactions, I have been able to refine much of what is written here, and I am grateful to them for their contributions.

None of the work here is original. Over the years I have picked up ideas from many sources, and have tried them out on groups of students and ministers. I hope that I have acknowledged all the written influences in the text.

All quotations from the Bible, unless otherwise indicated, are from the Good News Bible.

Two people have helped me with the production of this book, and I am grateful to them both for their efficiency and interest. Sue Anderton was my secretary while most of it was being written, and she typed the majority of the text. Jan Tindale replaced her in the closing stages of writing, and she also has typed a substantial proportion.

My wife Gillian, and our three children, Matthew, Catherine, and Rachel, have all been constructive listeners to my sermons over many years. Their love and support have enabled me to write this book, and I owe them more thanks than words can express.

INTRODUCTION

HOW TO USE THIS BOOK

This book is not intended to be a theoretical discussion of the nature of preaching, but is, rather, a practical handbook aiming to help people through the steps of thinking about, preparing, and delivering sermons.

It can be used in different ways, either by individuals or by groups. The book has been designed so that if you start at the beginning and work through the chapters, treating each chapter as a lesson, it will build up into a complete course of preaching. Each chapter contains a number of exercises to help you to think about and put into practice the ideas and principles which are discussed. Most of these exercises can be done by someone working alone, but they are more effective if done in a group so that the results of thinking or practising can be discussed.

The book can also be dipped into at will. Each chapter is free standing, so if you need to begin with voice exercises, and then move on to ethical topics, you can do so. The exercises in each chapter are essential, and they will take some time to complete properly. This book is not, therefore, designed to be read straight through. It would be most useful if one chapter is read each week and the associated exercises completed before moving on.

Brief notes are given at the end of each chapter referring to books quoted. Full bibliographical details are given at the end of the book.

Part One

Why Preach?

1 THE PURPOSE OF PREACHING

Many of the audience on this occasion felt, as one John Nelson, that every word was addressed personally and directly to themselves. Nelson, a stonemason, has left a recollection of Wesley preaching in the upper Moorfields: "As soon as he got up on the stand he stroked back his hair and turned his eyes upon me. His countenance struck such an awful dread upon me, before I heard him speak, that it made my heart beat like the pendulum of a clock; and when he did speak, I thought his whole discourse was aimed at me." Yet, when Wesley had done, Nelson continues, "I said, 'This man can tell the secrets of my heart: he hath not left me there; for he hath showed the remedy, even the blood of Jesus.' "[1]

When we mount the pulpit steps to begin a sermon, what precisely do we think we are doing? Unless we begin by attempting to clarify the aims of preaching, we shall probably produce aimless and disconnected rambles which merely fill the time.

It is frequently suggested that preaching at the end of the twentieth century is considerably more difficult than it has been at any time in the past. The following may be among the reasons for this.

- The long tradition of oratory which has sustained preaching is dead.
- Contemporary men and women have a short concentration span, and rarely listen to long, uninterrupted speeches.
- The preacher has intense competition from television and other forms of entertainment.
- People no longer trust words. The politician, the journalist, and the advertising copywriter have all devalued the currency of language.

How do we cope with this apparent devaluation of the act of preaching? There is a variety of possible responses.

1. We can simply ignore the problem, and conduct our business as usual, trying to continue proclaiming what we consider to be the enduring Christian certainties without relating them to the difficulties of faith in the contemporary secular world. If in doubt, shout more loudly.
2. We can compromise by retreating from the traditional sermon and producing a brief chat. In this we can reinforce our own and the congregation's opinions, and decline to issue any uncomfortable challenges.
3. We can enter into a conspiracy of silence between the pulpit and the pew. When this happens the congregation does not ask the difficult questions of how all this gospel message relates to their ordinary lives; and the preacher does not address the implication of the gospel for jobs, family life, economics, etc. Instead of the good news, we can be caught in the trap of offering only an internalised spiritual message.

If we reject these as parodies of preaching, we need to ask the question of precisely what preaching is. To stand in the pulpit and talk about just anything is clearly not preaching. My opinions about life, politics, morality, or even religion and spirituality, are not preaching. I recently heard a sermon about ashing (the ceremonial imposition of ash on the foreheads of worshippers on Ash Wednesday). It explained how the ancient custom had grown up in the church, and how it had been developed. The sermon then stopped. What was missing? There was no announcement of the good news, no proclamation of the gospel, no application to the lives of the worshippers and, most surprisingly in such a context, no call to repentance.

Perhaps it is easier to begin with trying to define what preaching is not. It is not:

- insight into the preacher's own experience;
- a reinforcement of the political status quo;
- a criticism of the political status quo;
- general moral advice;
- a commentary on the liturgy.

Each of these elements may have their place in preaching, but none of them is its main thrust, and the preacher who habitually concentrates on one of these clearly is not fulfilling the task that has been set.

Can we, then, say anything positive about the role of preaching in our contemporary age? Many twentieth-century theologians, including some of those classed as radical, have placed surprisingly high value on the activity of preaching.

Karl Barth asserts that God acts among us as he acted in the narratives of the Bible. Through preaching we are brought into the presence of the eternal word of God in action. God's word is creative – it makes things happen. Preaching is the reannouncing of the word, and therefore we should expect to be encountered by the living God in the experience of preaching. Furthermore, the Church is created where a group of people respond in faith to the announcement of the word in the activity of preaching.

Rudolf Bultmann describes the confrontation with the crucified Lord which is brought about through preaching. This confrontation demands decision. The preacher is a herald whose proclamation brings forth a response, a decision for or against commitment. Using existential philosophy, Bultmann argues that the whole pattern of human existence depends upon the way we respond to the demands of the gospel.

Paul Tillich suggests that the preacher correlates the questions raised by human existence with the answers given in the gospel. Listening and answering are of equal importance in the preaching enterprise. The task of preaching is to discern what lies at the depths of human questioning, and to show how this is answered in the divine presence.

Each of these theologians is trying to provide a theological basis for the activity of preaching. They see it as much more fundamental than simply addressing a congregation and trying to improve their religious faith. Barth, Bultmann and Tillich in different ways see the preaching activity to be bound up with God's activity in the contemporary world.

PREACHING IN THE NEW TESTAMENT

Although it is important to understand how preaching has been viewed in recent times, any analysis of the nature of the sermon must begin with the public ministry of Jesus himself. Whatever one's view of the historical reliability of the New Testament material, whether conservative fundamentalist or radical critic, it is clear that preaching and teaching formed a central part of Jesus' activity.

Mark's Gospel opens with John who "appeared in the desert, baptising and preaching. 'Turn away from your sins and be baptised,' he told the people, 'and God will forgive your sins.' " (Mark 1.4). This is followed almost immediately by Jesus himself developing the message of John, and announcing the primary purpose of his mission. "After John had been put in prison, Jesus went to Galilee and preached the good news from God. 'The right time has come,' he said, 'and the Kingdom of God is near. Turn away from your sins and believe the good news.' " (Mark 1.14).

In Mark we find that a common pattern develops. Jesus proclaims a divine event, often linked with a healing or exorcism. This is followed by an invitation or challenge to respond with repentance and belief. Here is the basic pattern of Christian preaching which is to persist throughout the centuries. An event takes place which demonstrates God's saving action in his world; a challenge is issued which must be worked out in the response of the individual and the community. The event may be in the past or in the present; the response must be in the present and the future. The present and future elements are both vital – a message purely about the past is not the good news of the gospel.

Mark (3.14) and Luke (9.2) both report Jesus as giving the task of preaching to his disciples. After the resurrection and the gift of the Holy Spirit, the early Church sees preaching as its highest priority. Peter's proclamation in Acts 2.14–39 sets a pattern for this task. The shape of this address by Peter is as follows:

1. introduction – verses 14–15;
2. recalling of prophecy – verses 16–21;
3. proclamation of the events of Jesus' life, death and resurrection – verses 22–35;
4. challenge to acknowledge the significance of these events – verse 36;
5. invitation to commitment and the Christian life – verses 38–39.

A similar scheme can be seen in other sermons in Acts, and these passages should be studied.

> ### *Exercise*
>
> Read the following passages and break them down into sections. You could use the scheme suggested above, or devise your own.
>
> Acts 3.11–26
> Acts 7.2–53
>
> Contrast these with the shape of Paul's address in Acts 17.22–31. How does the pattern of this sermon differ? Why does it differ?

A recent report from a commission of the Methodist church gave some indication of the range of elements involved in preaching, and this should warn us against accepting too simplistic a definition.

> *Most sermons involve an element of Christian teaching. This may mean the exposition of a text or a passage of scripture. The treatment of a particular Christian belief, consideration of the Christian response to an aspect of life. However, the sermon is far more than an educational exercise. It should be judged on its effectiveness as a means of grace rather than on its educational value. Preaching is not simply a teaching activity. It is a proclamatory event, in which people are invited to respond to the good news. Preaching is one of God's chosen ways for renewing apostolic faith from one generation to the next. Preaching is the Church confessing its faith; so that the word becomes again the living word of God.*[2]

We may now be able to sketch tentatively some possible definitions of preaching. Consider each of the following sentences, and comment on how strongly you agree or disagree with each of them. At the end add a definition or definitions of your own.

Preaching is:

1. telling the story of the saving acts of God in Christ;
2. challenging people to repentance and commitment;
3. exposition of the Bible;

4. teaching people how to live a Christian life in the contemporary world;
5. a way of ensuring that individuals in the congregation believe in the right way;
6. the sharing of personal experiences and opinions about life and faith;
7. a way of handing on the Christian tradition.

Our underlying theology of preaching, whether explicit or implicit, will determine our view of the role of the preacher. There are a number of possible models for the preacher's task. The following are drawn from some of the more traditional understandings of the task of the preacher.

1. **Apostle** – The preacher is a person sent by God with a task to perform.
2. **Herald** – The preacher is to announce what God has done, frequently to an unresponsive audience.
3. **Prophet** – The preacher is to interpret society in the light of God's word, which may involve announcing divine judgement.
4. **Interpreter** – The preacher is to translate the insights of the Bible so that they can be appropriated and used in day-to-day lives.
5. **Witness** – The preacher is to testify to events which he or she has personal knowledge of.

Exercises

1. Try to describe how you understand the activity of preaching to be a part of God's ongoing activity within his creation.
2. Comment on the list of possible definitions of preaching (1–7) above.
3. If you are working in a group, come to an agreed definition of preaching.

Notes

1. Taken from *The English Sermon*, vol. 3, Robert Nye (ed.), 1750–1850, pp. 34–5.
2. From the Methodist Commission on Worship, sections 46–7.

2 WHO IS THE SERMON FOR?

Before starting to prepare a sermon, proper consideration should be given to whom is to listen. Too frequently, preachers speak without giving thought to the make-up and needs of the congregation. It would obviously be both insensitive and inappropriate to give the same address to a family service in which the congregation contains a large number of toddlers and to twenty retired people at a quiet 8 a.m. Book of Common Prayer eucharist. One of the preliminary questions on every preacher's mind should be, "What are the needs, wants and expectations of these people?"

The danger is that we preach mainly for ourselves. We may preach to gain self-esteem, to be approved of, or simply because we like the sound of our own voices.

It is all very well to assert that the sermon should be appropriate to its listeners, but how in practice do we decide what is appropriate? How do we determine what they need to hear, and what they are capable of receiving?

It is essential to find a method of listening to those to whom you preach. This should be relatively easy for the full-time minister, who will have regular day-to-day pastoral contact with a large proportion of the people for whom the minister leads worship, and thus will hear questions raised every day which could form the basis of preaching. Even so, it will still be necessary to give some time to listening carefully to issues which are live for the congregation and which need to be addressed in sermons, and to receive feedback on sermons which you have preached.

Try the following as ways of keeping in touch with those to whom you preach.

- Call together a group of people from the congregation who will help you prepare a sermon, or series of addresses. The group can study Bible passages together, and raise issues which are to be preached about. The sermon is then based on the discussion.
- After a sermon has been preached, invite a group of people to discuss it with you, perhaps over coffee after the service.

- Occasionally have a "request a sermon" Sunday. The week before, members of the church could put written requests into a box, and the preacher could choose one or more topics to address.

Each of these methods helps the preacher to keep in touch with the listeners, but they should be used only occasionally because any method used to excess soon becomes stale.

DIFFERENT TYPES OF CONGREGATION

The Group

Exercise

As an aid to drawing up a profile of a congregation, take a few minutes to write a description of the congregation in your own church. If there is more than one type of service offered regularly, describe each of the groups. Your description should contain most of the following information:

- number of people;
- age structure;
- occupations;
- newspapers read;
- educational experience;
- Christian experience;
- members' leisure interests;
- burning community issues.

You may wish to add other ways of describing the congregation to this list, and some of the items might need explanation: for example, it is important to find out which newspapers are read by members of the congregation. This gives you some insight not only into their likely view of the world, and to some extent their political outlook, but also into the ideas and language they will feel happy with. If you are a preacher who reads the *Guardian*, and takes its attitudes and language for granted, you should not be surprised if a congregation who are predominantly *Sun* readers do not follow your sermons.

It is vital that you should listen to the main issues which occupy the community. Perhaps parents are campaigning for a safer road crossing outside the local school; perhaps the local psychiatric hospital is closing; perhaps a bail hostel is about to open in the neighbourhood. If the majority of the people are concentrating on these things, the preacher must ask whether or not to address them in the light of the gospel.

The Individuals

Another way of bearing in mind the "target audience" for a sermon is to think of specific people within the congregation, and to ask whether the sermon relates to them. Do not, however, make the mistake of aiming an address at someone. Preaching should not be a vehicle for making an individual pastoral or moral point, and it certainly should not be used for criticizing individuals.

Exercises

1. Pick out some individuals in your church, and write a paragraph describing them as people. Can you suggest what they need to hear in sermons?
2. In general terms, how might sermons differ for the following groups? Suggest four characteristic elements which you should include in a sermon in each of the following contexts.
   (a) A family service on Mothering Sunday, containing many children and their parents. A large proportion of the congregation attend church only occasionally.
   (b) A Sunday evening preaching service in a small village chapel, with a congregation of two dozen, all over the age of 60.
   (c) A large student congregation in a college chapel.

Cold Preaching

There will inevitably be times when you address a group of people with whom you have had no previous contact. Even a few minutes before the service you can be usefully making contacts. Speak to some of the worshippers as they arrive – this will give you a feel for your listeners, and it will mean that those with whom you have spoken will instinctively feel some point of contact with you. Take a little time to read their church magazine and weekly news-sheet, and, if possible, allude to an item from them in your sermon. If you know some members of the congregation, phone one of them a few days before your sermon, and ask one or two questions about the current concerns of the church, what is being discussed in house groups, and so on.

WHY DON'T SERMONS HAVE MORE EFFECT – A THEORY

The frequent gap between preachers' understanding of what they believe they are teaching, and the apparent lack of learning and appropriation of that teaching by the people in the churches, raises a number of puzzling questions. At first sight it might simply appear that the church and its preachers are dismally bad at teaching. No doubt this is part of the picture. The person who preaches for twenty minutes on Sunday and imagines that the congregation is thereby being taught is clearly living in ignorance of the way people actually learn. But even those churches which give time and effort to constructing groups, and which achieve a reasonable degree of success in attracting members to teaching activities, do little better. Many lay people who have attended study groups for years are scarcely able to give an intelligent account of their faith. Is all the time given to such activities by the leaders of local churches simply being wasted?

In his book *What Prevents Christian Adults from Learning?*, John Hull has given serious thought to this problem. In an analysis of contemporary thought, he suggests that religion is seen as a haven: "It is valued precisely because there one can escape from the problems and demands which crowd in upon us from the newspapers and the television" (p. 7). This religious haven is closely linked with the idealized haven of childhood, for "as parents and adults we socialise our children into that for which we have fond nostalgia, but can no longer take seriously for ourselves. Deep in their hearts, many people believe that religion is really for children" (p. 8). In this simplified and nostalgic state of mind, learning would be confusing, and would violate the simplicity of the haven. It would demand a painful reassessment of the way the world is seen, and so is avoided.

Hull follows this with a number of important points about the difficulty which the Church finds in educating lay people in the Christian faith. Most congregations are, he rightly suggests, "a mere collection of individuals who happen to meet together in order to do together what they could with almost equal effectiveness do alone." Not only, then, is there an inbuilt resistance to British Christians meeting together to learn about the faith, there is also a deeply passive attitude on the part of almost all laity. Many churches have "a strong tradition of lay passivity due partly to the reservation of sacramental functions for the priest" (p. 17). Thus, if they are to be educated about changing patterns of ministry, or about the basic facts of the faith, a drastic shift in the way clergy and lay people relate to one another may be needed, at least in the traditional churches.

At the root of the problem, Hull suggests, is that "religious commitment may be a form of ideological enclosure" (p. 47). By this he means that one's beliefs can form a protective barrier against the more distasteful aspects of the modern world, and provide access to the half-remembered time of childhood, when one was protected from reality by parents, other adults, and by one's fantasies. If those beliefs are threatened or questioned, then the barrier is erected. Thus, adult Christian learning is not just a matter of "studying what the New Testament has to say about baptism, or what the early church practised, but also involves a shift in the very quality of the belief system itself" (p. 51). Learning about the faith is painful because it involves a change of assumptions and lifestyle, and yet one believes in order to retreat into a former lifestyle and to avoid the change which is taking place all around.

Hull then draws attention to the difficulty of articulating beliefs and feelings which are deeply held. Indeed, the more committed a person is to certain beliefs and feelings, the more difficult it becomes to talk about them, and therefore to engage in educational exercises which might challenge or change them. "People's ability to speak clearly about their ideas and feelings and beliefs decreases as thcsc bccomc morc important, more central to the inner life" (p. 54). To be made to think about these beliefs is actually distressing, and so ideological walls are erected from within whose safety adherents may "go on sorties or excursions into the hostile world beyond" (p. 128). Within these walls, "It is enough to believe that somebody knows that answer. This is more important than actually knowing the answer" (p. 135).

In an illuminating passage, Hull comments on the phenomenon of "sermon–deafness", when lay people will say firmly that their minister is a good preacher, but are unable to relate anything about the contents of the sermons.

> *One cannot help noticing again and again in British churches that a preacher who speaks in simple, emotive rhetoric with a warm flow of stereotypes is preferred to a preacher who makes a genuine effort to tackle some real aspect of contemporary Christian life and faith. The preacher, most congregations seem to feel, should not make these kinds of demands upon his listeners. No matter how well educated and successful, they may complain of not being able to understand a preacher who encourages them to think, but the one who gives them a cosy feeling of being in a warm, familiar cocoon of accepted beliefs is admired and appreciated. It does not matter to the listeners that they are unable to repeat even the main theme of the sermon five minutes later; the important thing is the comforting emotion of familiarity and belonging which swept over them as they were listening to him. It is this which many church people seem to be referring to when they speak of worship and what it means to them. [p. 65]*

This analysis undoubtedly has much to commend it, and perhaps much of the difficulty Hull describes is caused by a lack of clarity about the purpose of preaching. If we were to understand it as a means of exhortation and encouragement, then the effect of which Hull writes would not be seen as so undesirable. If, however, we imagine that sermons are about conveying information, then perhaps they are doomed to failure. The question which needs to be asked is how, if we think it desirable to make Christians better informed about their faith, can we so alter their attitudes that they will want to learn?

Hull's thesis is directly applicable, for example, to the furore caused by J. A. T. Robinson's *Honest to God*, and by the controversy aroused by David Jenkins's views on the virgin birth and resurrection. When the population at large discovered that these two church leaders were asking questions about the nature of Christian belief in general, and about the content of specific beliefs, unease and condemnation were widespread. If Hull is right, the unease was caused by the mere fact that questions were being raised about topics which most people are unable to question. For the first time, some people were being made to face up to the possibility that questions could be asked about the central beliefs of the resurrection and the incarnation, and this in itself caused disquiet more than the actual content of the statements or writings. The task of church leaders, people seemed to say, was to confirm them in their beliefs, not to make them examine their faith.

Exercise

Do you think Hull is correct in his analysis of what prevents Christians from learning? What evidence do you have which might support or refute his views? Do you want to restate your definition of a sermon in light of what he says?

3 PREACHING AND CULTURE

The Church needs to seek for and to identify vehicles (signs and symbols) suited to the celebration of the spiritual experiences of those outside her boundaries. She needs to look within contemporary culture for the symbols of grief, of joy, of reaching beyond, that are apt for her. The Church should seek to build on those vehicles which others use to handle their more significant experiences. She needs also to reinterpret her own symbols so that she can both acquire and offer new and deeper insights into contemporary culture. In this way the living God can bring new life both to the Church and to the community at large.[1]

Preachers must consider their listeners not only as individuals, but also as members of a society and of a variety of communities. People come to worship not as blank sheets of paper waiting for us to write on them. They bring with them many things which will impinge on how they hear and receive the gospel. Perhaps the most important of these is language; the words and concepts the preacher and hearers share, and which enable the process of communication to take place. Almost as important as language is the bundle of interconnected, and often unspoken, elements which make up a common culture. This includes politics, philosophy, outlook, values and ways of behaviour. On a less abstract level, this cultural common ground is expressed in television and other mass media, in the sub-groups of which we are members (including the Church), and in our practical morality.

The biblical writers also shared a culture (or perhaps a variety of cultures), and a central task for the preacher is to ask how the gap between New Testament cultures and our own culture can be bridged. If we are to help people to hear the gospel, we must be aware that it has to be proclaimed to them in words and ideas which they are able to appropriate. This means listening to and understanding the assumptions with which our hearers live and work in their daily lives.

One of the earliest, and perhaps the most important, ventures of cultural interpretation was that undertaken in the first generation of the Church, and is seen within the New Testament. At his conversion, Paul acquired an understanding of Jesus' death which was expressed in the sacrificial language of Judaism. His problem was that this language, and the ideas which lay behind it, were incomprehensible to those who were not grounded in the Jewish faith. There would have been little point explaining the cross to his non-Jewish audiences in terms of Old Testament sacrifice – it would have made no sense. Paul's solution was to express the sacrifice of Jesus in ideas which his hearers could comprehend. The Roman empire was held together by its understanding of law, so Paul reinterpreted the central Christian event in terms of the court-room. Instead of preaching about sacrifice, he wrote about Christians being put right with the eternal law of God, and used a court-room word – justification – to explain the atonement. Like Paul, our task is to seek ways of expressing the heart of the gospels in symbols and analogies which remain true to the revelation, and which also work for our contemporaries.

We need to begin by addressing the question of how the gospel and our culture relate to each other. There are a number of possible views about the relationship, including the following.

1. Late twentieth-century western European culture is antagonistic towards the gospel, and we must preach "against" it.
2. Our culture is generally supportive of the gospel, and we can use many of its assumptions and customs in our proclamation.
3. Our culture is neutral, and neither aids nor hinders our preaching.
4. Culture is irrelevant – we simply proclaim the gospel irrespective of the assumptions of our hearers.
5. Gospel and culture both have their place in the life of a contemporary Christian, so we need to ensure that a healthy dialogue is taking place between the two.

Exercise

Either individually, or as a group, decide which of the above options most clearly reflects your view.

Some people take the view that the preacher operates in a culture which in its deepest assumptions is anti-Christian. As Neville Clark puts it, "cultural static may be blocking out the hearing of the word of God".[2] There are two levels on which this "cultural static" may be operating.

The first level, and the easier to grasp, is that of the images with which we are confronted. Television serves us a diet of violence, overt sexuality, and mistrust of authority. The advertisements portray a world in which there is no pain or struggle, and in which everyone has all that they want. Against this background, the preacher's message seems out of touch and irrelevant. If modern society is spurred on by market forces and covetousness, the gospel has nothing to contribute.

There is also a deeper, more philosophical, level at which culture may be operating against Christianity. Lesslie Newbigin, in his book *Foolishness to the Greeks*, argues that the assumptions of the philosophical movement of the eighteenth century usually called the Enlightenment have led to a separation between facts and values in our culture. Facts are those things which are publicly observable and testable, and include the findings of science, technology, and economics. Values are private, and are the outcome of the individual's preferences, and so cannot be determined by public discussion. Religion and morality belong, in the prevailing philosophy, to the internal, private world of values. A person's religious preferences, therefore, have no bearing on the public world, and are merely to do with his or her own inner choices.

If Newbigin is correct in his analysis, and his writing seems to have gained widespread acceptance, there is a serious problem for the preacher to address. Are we content to target our sermons at the inner world of personal and spiritual values, or do we believe that the gospel is also to be proclaimed in the public world of facts?

An alternative view of the position outlined above is that western culture is generally positive towards the Christian gospel, and that the assumptions of our society aid the preacher's task. Those who take this line of argument would point to the freedom of speech and conscience which is enjoyed in western Europe and North America, to the openness and tolerance which is enshrined in law and constitution, and (especially in England) to the relationship between the churches and the establishment. Religious programmes are regularly broadcast on television and radio, religious books are openly on sale and widely bought, and

Christian worship and instruction is practised in many schools. All these elements point to a culture in which religious choice and commitment is openly acknowledged, and in which information about the Christian faith is freely available.

Perhaps it would be better to argue that our culture is "religiously neutral". The task of government in a free society is to create a climate in which what constitutes the good life is left to individual decision. Thus, religious and moral commitment (or lack of it) is neither encouraged nor discouraged, but is entirely at the citizen's choice. If this is the case, we must recognize that the prevailing view represents a significant departure from most societies in history, and in particular from the assumptions which lay behind the New Testament. The debates between the infant Christian faith, Judaism, and the Roman empire which we overhear taking place in the New Testament all assume that religious commitment is the norm. The protagonists are arguing about what form of commitment is correct. Should one follow the way of Jesus, or of the Pharisees, or of the gods of Rome? Our situation is entirely different, for we are trying to present religious commitment to a society in which individuals can choose whether or not to commit themselves to any faith.

Exercise

Which of these positions do you find yourself most in sympathy with? What evidence can you use to support your view?

We have been talking so far as if people live in a single "culture". In reality, each of us inhabits a number of separate, sometimes overlapping, sub-cultures. The same person might live with his family in a small village, commute to his place of work in a large city, watch football on Saturday, visit a gym in his lunch hour, and be a member of the Labour party. Each of these places and activities has its own language, traditions, and accepted ways of behaviour. In each, the person will be fulfilling a different role.

There are also broader sub-cultures which are easily identifiable. Various ethnic groupings share distinct life-styles, languages, and even religions. Young people are identifiable in terms of dress, purchasing patterns, and again language, for they have their own slang words which seem to change almost from month to month, and which can only be understood by their peers.

In these terms, Christianity can be described as a sub-culture alongside others. Those who regularly attend church have a language, a common pattern of behaviour when assembled, often a similar way of dressing, and so on. The danger in our multi-cultured society, is that the Christian sub-culture is seen as just another choice, no more and no less important than membership of the Women's Institute, the golf club, or a political party. Because each sub-culture tends to be self-contained, what one does in one grouping does not impinge upon the others, and is kept in a discrete compartment.

Further, it seems that many churches, perhaps the majority of churches in Britain, inhabit a particular general sub-culture, and this limits their appeal to a small sector of the population. Consider the following quotation, and ask whether it is an accurate description of the majority of people in our churches:

> *Relative affluence is not the only distinguishing feature of the professional classes in a modern society. Theirs is a sub-culture characterised by intellectual, rational and academic approaches to the problems confronting them. The written word is their chief form of communication. Such intellectual devices are not employed by the majority in this country.*[3]

Exercise

Draw up a list of the sub-cultures of which you are a member. Choose one of them, and describe its particular language, traditions, and patterns of behaviour.

Our problem is how to proclaim that Christianity is not a separate sub-culture, but is involved in, indeed is the foundation of, all human life. If we preach only about inner spiritual experience, we should not be surprised to find that our hearers have difficulty relating their Christian faith to the other groups of which they are members – the family, work place, or leisure activity.

Notes

1. From *Good News in our Times*, Church House Press, p. 85.

2. Neville Clark, *Preaching in Context*, p. 12.

3 *Good News in Our Times*, p. 21.

Part Two

Bible and Sermon

4 CHOOSING THE TEXT

The Vicar of Brighton, seeing his son pouring away the family fortune on extraordinary church buildings preached from the text, "Lord have mercy on my son, for he is a lunatic". It was a time when texts were much used in this way and it is recounted that once after some trouble Father Wagner sacked both his curates. The departing curate preached on the text, "Stay ye here with the ass, while I and the lad go yonder".[1]

Before we can look at the process of working from biblical text towards a finished sermon, we must ask the apparently simple question of how we decide which passage of scripture to base the sermon on. Just occasionally, we may wish to preach a sermon which does not directly relate to a biblical passage, for instance when addressing an ethical topic or other contemporary issue, and this is dealt with in Chapter 13, Social and Moral Topics.

There are three main ways of deciding upon the text:

1. through prayer and waiting for inspiration;
2. by following a lectionary;
3. by first choosing a topic to preach upon, then finding a biblical passage to fit with it.

Exercise

Take a few minutes to note down the strengths and weaknesses of each of these methods of choice.

While the first and third methods undoubtedly have their place within the scheme of preaching, and will be more firmly adhered to in some church traditions than others, there are considerable advantages to using a lectionary as the normal method of choosing the passage with which to work. In 1967 the Joint Liturgical Group, consisting of representatives from all the main Christian denominations in Great Britain, published a common lectionary, and this underlies the lectionaries used in the *Methodist Service Book*, the *United Reformed Church Service Book*, and the Church of England's *Alternative Service Book.* The readings chosen are centred on the two main Christian festivals of Christmas and Easter, and in each cycle there is a time of preparation, the celebration of the festival itself, and a period of reflection of the significance of the events afterwards. The knowledge that other major churches in Britain are using the same sets of scripture readings each week has done much to bring the churches closer together.

Basing one's preaching on this, or a similar lectionary, has the following advantages.

1. It ensures that over a period of time the preacher covers all the main Christian themes, and it gives shape and coherence to the preaching.
2. It forces you to preach on passages of scripture which you might not otherwise choose. There are great dangers in choosing each week what to preach on, because it might lead to always speaking about your own favourite passages. This may lead to the congregation being fed a very restricted diet of biblical passages.
3. The congregation can know in advance which passages will be used as the basis for the sermon, and can read them in advance of the service. It is, therefore, possible for them to come to worship more prepared and receptive.

The disadvantages of slavishly following a set plan of readings may be as follows.

1. It tends to stifle inspiration, because the preacher is restricted to pre-determined themes.
2. The set passages of scripture may not be suitable for special events or for particular Sundays in your local church's calendar. For example, you may have invited local schools to take part in a service, and find that the lectionary readings do not provide a good starting point for worship with children.
3. Many important contemporary moral issues are not directly addressed in scripture, and would not be raised by the ordinary round of readings. If you wish to preach about genetic

engineering, animal rights, conservation, or nuclear power, you will want to choose very carefully the passages of scripture which are to be read.

4. The set lectionaries for Sundays do not include the whole of scripture, and although all major biblical themes are covered, there are significant passages which are omitted. There is, for example, little in the Joint Liturgical Group lectionary on the history of Israel, and the Joseph stories are not represented at all.

> ***Exercise***
>
> Do you agree with this list of advantages and disadvantages of using a lectionary? Can you think of other points on either side of the debate?

If you are preaching in a church which does not follow a lectionary, or you do not wish to follow it, then you must develop methods of ensuring that your preaching does not become restricted to your favourite few passages. The congregation which is fed only by a preacher who makes a limited choice of Bible passages is living on a very restricted diet, and is not being exposed to the great riches of scripture. There is clearly value in leaving yourself open to the inspiration of the Spirit when preparing to preach, but it is unlikely that the preacher who continually returns to the same six chapters of scripture is hearing the Spirit aright.

We all make a selection of what we consider to be the most important parts of scripture, however unconsciously. Do you feel yourself drawn to preach more often on Romans than on James, more frequently on Luke than on Matthew, on Amos than on Hosea? If this is the case, reflect for a few moments on why your own theological position leads you in this way.

It is possible to guard against too narrow a choice, even when not following a lectionary, by adopting the following methods.

1. Occasionally preach a series of sermons in which you use a whole book of the Bible. You will then have to deal with sections you would not normally choose.

2. Make sure that you address the major festivals of the Christian year – Christmas, Easter, Pentecost, Advent – and choose readings which tell the stories of these festivals.
3. When you come across a passage in your own reading or study that you find difficult, preach about it. This will guard against you neglecting the parts of the Bible you find uncongenial.

Exercise

Suggest other methods you might follow for ensuring that you preach from a broad range of biblical texts.

Notes

1. From Colin Stephenson, *Merrily on High*, 1971.

5 USING THE BIBLE IN PREACHING

> *The religious imperative at any age is born at the intersection of the timeless and the time bound. We must not lose our ability to hear, across the generations, the transcendent voice of revelation: that is the argument against liberalism. But neither may we apply the text of revelation as if nothing significant had changed in the human situation in the intervening years: that is the argument against extremism. Liberalism grants too much to the present, extremism too much to the past. Against both, the task of the sage, prophet or religious philosopher has always been to mediate between the two, between ancient texts and present contexts, the former determining our aspirations, the latter, their field of application.*[1]

Clearly the Bible must be a central factor in preaching, whatever the Christian tradition within which the preacher stands. An essential question must be how the preacher moves from text to sermon. Whatever mechanism is used to choose a biblical text, whether it be personal inspiration or relying on a lectionary, there is still the question of how the text becomes a preached sermon. The view which the preacher takes of scripture will to some extent determine how it is used in preaching. The following views of scripture all have consequences for the sermon.

1. All scripture has a meaning for today, and if the preacher is only faithful enough, or intelligent enough, or receptive enough, then the meaning will be made plain. The preacher's task is then to expound scripture in such a way that the congregation can appropriate the meaning as their own. Preachers who take this view of the Bible often end up using considerable amounts of allegory in their preaching, for it is the only way they can find of basing sermons on the more obscure passages.

2. The second view is that scripture contains statements of divine truth, and that the task of the preacher is to expound these statements, and to apply them to today. In effect, the Bible is viewed as a textbook of doctrines.
3. The third view is that, lying behind scripture, there is a witness to the great actions of God in history. Those preachers who take this view will attempt to describe the main themes of scripture and to draw attention to the divine actions lying behind them.
4. Some preachers regard large parts of scripture as morally or theologically inadequate, and are happy to leave out these portions and never to use them in preaching. Those within this tradition might commonly appeal to scripture's authority in general theological and moral terms, rather than relying on it as revealing specific timeless ideas or truths.

Whatever view of scripture is taken, it is almost certain that all preachers will have their favourite passages, and leave large sections out of their consideration. The danger of this is that favourite passages are used continually, and the preacher is not compelled to struggle with the parts of scripture which are found uncongenial. The task of integrating one's view of various parts of scripture is demanding, and it is not therefore surprising that almost all preachers make an unconscious selection.

Perhaps the most important piece of advice in moving from text to the sermon, is that the Bible passages should be read, prayed over, and studied, some time in advance of the sermon. The person who does not read the Bible passages for tomorrow's sermon until Saturday evening is unlikely to have time to give sufficient study and consideration to those passages. Random thoughts on the passage are not enough. There must be a genuine attempt both to expound the original meaning of the text, and also to relate it to the present day. However good the preacher's knowledge, a straightforward lecture on the text is not a sermon. It only becomes a sermon when the meaning of the text is related to the Christian life and experience of those to whom it is being preached.

Do not be surprised if, on the first reading, the text does not spark off ideas for a sermon. They may come as you look at a commentary, or perhaps as a result of reading a newspaper or watching a television programme, or as you mull over the readings for a few days. There can be no rules on gaining inspiration; it is the work of the Holy Spirit.

The centre of the sermon must be searching for the meaning of the passage in today's world. Professor Leonard Hodgson formulated a classic question: "What must the truth be now if people who thought as they did put it like that?" In other words, how can the truth which is expressed in the scriptural text be seen to be truth for our age, bearing in mind the huge cultural gap between the biblical world and our own time? The problem is not just one of language, we are not simply talking about translating from Hebrew or Greek into English. There is also the problem of translating the ideas from one culture into another culture.

As soon as you come up with an idea or series of ideas for the sermon, you must ask yourself the question – where is the gospel? We may be very keen on telling our congregations to work harder, to do more, to live better lives, to view the world through particular political spectacles. But at the heart of preaching is the proclamation of the gospel and, unless the good news is recognizable in the sermon, then the Word is not being preached.

FROM TEXT TO SERMON

Initially when we look at a passage which will form the basis of a sermon, we need to begin by deciding what sort of scriptural literature we are dealing with. Only when we come to some sort of decision about the nature of this passage can we move on to considering how to handle it within the sermon.

There is great variety of types of literature in the Bible, but passages set for preaching in the lectionaries are likely to fall into one of the following three categories.

Historical narrative

Begin by asking whether there are other accounts of the same incident within scripture, or even possibly in non-biblical literature. If so, what happens when we compare these accounts? Does it reveal something important about the perspective from which the writer is working? For example, the books of 1 and 2 Kings divide the monarchs very simply into the good and the bad. The criterion for the good is that they reigned longer. Their view of history is rather like old western films. So, if you are using Kings in preaching, you must be aware of their tendency to oversimplify the way good and evil work out in practice.

You need also to consider the context in which the passage is set. For example in 1 Samuel 15, Saul hacks to death the defenceless king Agag, before the Lord. Saul seems to have believed that false gods could be killed off if the people who served them were killed.

Perhaps the most useful approach to historical passages, particularly in the Old Testament, is to attempt to fit them into the overall biblical themes. Begin by asking how this passage fits into, for example, the covenant theme, the exodus theme, or the theme of God's activity within human history.

Myth

Myth is best understood as universal human truth expressed in the form of a dramatic narrative. It is a story about the experience of human faith. The meaning of the myth is not in the details of the story, but in the overall truth which the story enshrines. We must recognize that many of the major biblical myths touch our congregations at their deepest levels because of the universal character of such mythology.

The question to come to grips with when dealing with a piece of mythological writing is what is the central truth the writer is wrestling with. Avoid the temptation to be diverted by minor matters. For example, when dealing with the opening chapters of Genesis, we might be side-tracked by the question of why women experience pain in childbirth. The answer given by the writer of Genesis is that pain is a punishment for having taken a leading part in the fall of humanity. This, however, is not the major point of the myth – it is only a secondary detail.

We can follow up whether we have correctly discerned the main point of a mythological story by asking whether it is generally confirmed in the rest of scripture, and whether the theme seems to find echoes in the life and teaching of Jesus.

Gospel

We may wish to begin by looking at parallels in other gospels, particularly if we are dealing with synoptic material. This may show up the interests and concerns of the particular writer we are dealing with. For example, in Mark 10.46–52 Jesus heals a single blind beggar, whereas in Matthew 20.29–34, what is recognizably the same incident contains the healing of two blind beggars. The point may be that Jesus does not heal us in isolation but along with other members of our community. It could also be that for Matthew, writing within a primarily Jewish context, two witnesses made a valid testimony.

We should also ask to whom the original saying of Jesus in the gospel passage before us was directed and what its purpose was; was Jesus laying down legislation which is permanently binding on all disciples, or was he talking directly to his immediate contemporaries?[2]

Once we have determined our approach to the passage of scripture we are working with, and spent some time studying it in commentaries and reading it in other versions of the Bible, we need to develop a method of working towards the outline of a sermon. Some of the following steps may help.

1. Work through the passage and note down any key words which seem to you to be of theological or pastoral importance.
2. Does there seem to be a major theme underlying this passage?
3. Work through the passage again, jotting down any ideas which it sparks off in your mind. These may, or may not, be directly related to the text.
4. Is there any strong contemporary relevance in this passage? Does it obviously connect with something in the news, or with a current problem?
5. Go away and do something else. Ideally this period should last for about a week, during which time the passage can be working on your subconscious.
6. Begin to formulate an aim for the sermon. You should be able to summarize in a single sentence precisely what it is you want to say.
7. Sketch out a sequence of between three and six sub headings under which you will write specific passages on the sermon.
8. Write the sermon a paragraph at a time, sticking closely to your outline.
9. Rewrite the sermon, making sure that it hangs together as a coherent whole.

WORKING THROUGH A SERMON

The aim of this exercise is not to force your preaching into a mould, nor is it to stifle the action of the Spirit. It is, rather, to help develop a method which, at the very least, can be used when all other inspiration seems to have run dry. Sitting down at the desk with a blank piece of paper can be an unnerving experience. You must prepare a sermon for next Sunday; where do you begin? It undoubtedly helps to have a working pattern which will lead you through a series of steps towards the finished sermon.

Imagine that next Sunday is the ninth Sunday before Christmas in the lectionary. The readings set for the day are as follows:

- Genesis 2.4–9; 15–end
- Revelation 4
- John 3.1–8

Putting into practice some of the steps above, we might proceed like this. Begin by reading the passages carefully, preferably in more than one translation. The aim is to try and narrow down the material into a form which can realistically be addressed in a sermon, but at the same time to allow interesting and perhaps puzzling aspects of the passages to be emphasized.

Work through the passages, noting down any words or phrases which seem important. At the same time, note any questions you have which you might want to look up in commentaries or other sources.

With the passages above the exercise might go as follows.

Genesis 2

Verse 5 "The Lord had not sent any rain…" It is interesting here that the rain sent by God seems to be the catalyst of growth.

Verse 6 "Water would come up from beneath the surface and water the ground." Does this compare with the flood story later in Genesis? There may be connections here with other ancient cultures in which the seasonal flooding of the river ensures fertility (this was especially true of the Nile).

Verse 7 "Then the Lord God took some soil from the ground and formed a man out of it; he breathed life-giving breath into his nostrils and the man began to live." This seems to be the heart of the passage. It is interesting that it seems to suggest two parts to the man – the physical "soil from the ground", and the animating breath of life which comes from God. Is the writer describing an historical event, or is this a description of the creation of every person? Does a decision on this question affect the central message of the passage?

Verse 8 "Then the Lord God planted a garden." Why is a garden offered as the symbol of a pre-fall existence?

Verse 9 "The tree that gives life and the tree that gives knowledge of what is good and what is bad." What do these trees mean? What is the difference between the two? The help of commentaries is needed here.

Verse 18 "It is not good for the man to live alone." Why not? Because the nature of human beings is to exist in relationship?

Revelation 4

Verse 2 "Caught up by the Spirit." (*New English Bible* (NEB)) What does this mean? It seems to be a reminder of the passage in Ezekiel? Perhaps we should check the commentaries.

Verse 4 Who are the 24 elders? They are generally thought to be the fathers of the tribes of Israel, and the twelve apostles.

There seems to be a great wealth of imagery in this chapter. What is meant by the seven spirits of God? What is the symbolism of the sea of glass? The four living creatures seem to be symbolic of the four evangelists. The song in verse 8 is reminiscent of Isaiah chapter 6.

John 3

Verse 2 Why did Nicodemus visit Jesus at night? Presumably because he was afraid of being seen visiting a religious revolutionary?

Verse 3 "No one can see the Kingdom of God unless he is born again." This seems to be the centre of this story. Verse 5 must be a clear reference to baptism.

Verse 8 "The wind blows wherever it wishes." You remember that the same Hebrew word means spirit, breath and wind. There seem to be clear connections here with Genesis 1.2, "The Spirit of God hovered over the face of the water", (NEB) and the creation of the man in Genesis 2.7.

This is a collection of thoughts which arise from the set readings. There are clearly far too many points here for a sermon, so the next step is to narrow them down into a series of connected thoughts which can form the basis. After checking some questions in commentaries, and reading through your notes, you might decide on the following points as being particularly important.

1. In Genesis 2, you are attracted to the verse which describes God breathing life into the newly created man.
2. This easily links with two points in the gospel passage:
   (a) Jesus' assertion that one must be born again before seeing the Kingdom of God;
   (b) Verse 8, "The wind blows where it wills… so it is with the Spirit."

A number of possible illustrations come to mind:

- A baby's first breath immediately after birth, often followed by a loud cry. Do midwives really hold babies upside down and smack their bottoms?
- The restorative, recreative power of fresh air. Imagine walking on a seaside cliff, taking lungfuls of air and feeling like a new person.

- The invisible, seemingly fickle power of wind and its ability to do the unexpected, even the frightening.

Exercise

Draw these thoughts and illustrations together into a sermon outline. If you are working in a group, you could discuss ideas first, prepare the outlines individually, and then compare the results.

Notes

1. From Jonathan Sacks, *The Persistence of Faith*, p. 35.
2. The above paragraphs are much abbreviated from Richard Jones, *Groundwork of Worship and Preaching*, pp. 103–112.

6 PREACHING FROM THE OLD TESTAMENT

The Old Testament always has presented a problem to the Church and in general there have been three ways of attempting to solve it. First there was Marcion's way in the second century which was to eliminate it altogether. Christians who are Marcionites in this sense are not hard to find today. A second way of avoiding the difficulties was to spiritualise all that was read in the Old Testament leaving no stone unturned, to find types and analogies of Christ, moral values and homiletical advice, producing a result that was often fanciful in the extreme. A third way belongs to the late nineteenth and twentieth centuries; it consists generally in the theory of a progressive revelation in the Bible whereby the peak is reached in Christ with all that precedes it being regarded as inferior in the sense of being preparatory. Clearly on this view the Old Testament only possesses compelling interest for those studying the development of religion. It is of scant use for the preacher.[1]

It is rare to hear a good sermon preached using an Old Testament text as the basis. Some preachers openly admit that they find the Old Testament difficult, and so simply ignore it when preaching. They make a point which, on the surface, is valid – everything the Christian needs is contained within the New Testament, so why look outside its pages for sermon material? Others argue that the cultural differences between our world and that of the Old Testament are so great as to render the vast majority of it almost useless to the contemporary Christian. What possible benefit can be derived from incorporating rules for animal sacrifice into Christian thinking?

Against this, it can legitimately be asserted that the Christian Church through the centuries has insisted that the Old Testament is part of the totality of scripture. Attempts to excise parts of it in the past have been met with fierce, and successful, resistance. The Christian faith and the whole Bible are inseparable, and if the totality of the faith is to be preached to congregations, a satisfactory way of exploring and preaching on the Old Testament must be found.

Those preachers who do use the Old Testament regularly have often chosen to use it selectively. This selection may be unconscious, but is usually based on one of the following factors.

- Large sections of the Old Testament are ignored, and only the portions of it which easily fit into New Testament themes are used for sermons.
- Only the parts of the Old Testament which contain messianic material are drawn on, for it is then relatively easy to set them in a christological context.
- Incidents and individuals from the Old Testament are used as pegs on which to hang Christian doctrines or moral teaching.

It is easy to see that all the selective approaches outlined above fail to grapple with the Old Testament in its own right. Admittedly, we cannot as Christians read it in isolation from the New Testament and from Christian history, but to impose such a limited set of criteria on the scripture is to prevent ourselves from exploring its riches. We need, therefore, to derive a method of approaching the Old Testament as a preaching resource. This should avoid the common mistake of going to the text with a preconceived idea of what it ought to say and, instead, should allow it to speak for itself. This will involve the recognition that, however deep the cultural divide between ourselves and the ancient Hebrews appears to be, we are members of the same community of faith. They are in a real sense our spiritual ancestors, and we ignore what is in reality our own history at our peril. We can only come to an adequate understanding of our own position as a believing community within the world if we recognize the events and interpretations that have made us what we are.

One method of approach is to resist taking Old Testament figures as idealized Christians, glossing over their faults and ignoring their differences from us. If we regard them as real people struggling with faith, then we may be better able to relate their struggles to our own. Pretending that David was a perfect example of a devoted husband and father will not help the congregations to whom we preach gain an understanding of the way God uses less than perfect characters in his dealings with his chosen community. The more we enable people to recognize that in general the leading people in the Old Testament narrative had the same difficulties and faults as we do, the more this will facilitate their own reading of the Bible. Acknowledging that Jacob, Elijah, David, and the rest wrestled with doubts, lack of understanding, and temptations, and yet were still instruments of God's purpose, is one helpful way of handling the material.

It should, however, be realized that this method needs to be used carefully. In the historical and prophetic witness from which most of our "character studies" are likely to be taken, the primary focus is not on how God relates to individuals, but on how he deals with the whole community. These works are firstly about God's activity in public history, and only secondarily about his relationship with specific individuals. Those individuals may have a specific role in that history, and that role may have consequences for the development of their own faith, but the main point of the story is how God deals with his people as a corporate entity.

It is, perhaps, more constructive to approach preaching from Old Testament texts by looking at the different types of literature that can be found there, and by asking questions about what sort of message is intended in each type of literature. There are obviously some major genres of literature to be found in the Old Testament. The most significant are:

- law;
- prophecy;
- poetry;
- history;
- wisdom;
- mythology.

It seems obvious that, for example, a piece of poetry should not be treated as law, but it is surprising that such a mistake is made regularly from the pulpit. To address the question of the intention lying behind literature of the type you are dealing with is essential, and is the first step in allowing the text to speak for itself rather than having a preconceived interpretation imposed upon it.

On the basis of these principles, the following premises for preaching from the Old Testament may be suggested.

1. The God who reveals himself in the history of Israel is the God and Father of Jesus of Nazareth. As we have been integrated into the covenant made with Abraham, through the death and resurrection of Jesus, so the Old Testament is valid scripture for the Christian as well as for the Jew.

2. Scripture has been produced and transmitted by a community of believers, so it is not only a revelation of God, but also a reflection of the experience of the community of faith. So in scripture we have the voice of God and the voice of fellow believers side by side.

3. When, therefore, we preach on a text, we should first be asking not "What does this mean to me?", but "What has this meant to the believing community over the centuries?" We can then ask, "What does this continue to mean for us now?"

4. Scripture interprets scripture. In the Old Testament we hear the community of believers continuously reworking the central themes, especially exodus and covenant. Each time a theme is reworked, new questions are added about its relevance to contemporary society, and new insights are gained.

5. Because it is the product of the believing community, scripture is not static. It is, rather, continuously on the move. The preacher should therefore be looking for the direction in scripture, and should seek to interpret God's purposes in the history of the community, rather than concentrate on small scale issues.[2]

Exercise

Write outline sermon notes on one of the following passages. If you are working in a group, prepare different passages, and discuss both the process of developing the outlines and the results.

Exodus 12.1–14
Deuteronomy 10.12—11.1
1 Samuel 17.37–50
1 Kings 19.9–18
Isaiah 10.20–23
Job 42.1–6

Notes

1. D. W. Cleverley Ford, *New Preaching From the Old Testament*, p. ix.

2. These points are summarized and adapted from Donald Gowan, *Reclaiming the Old Testament for the Christian Pulpit*, pp. 8–9.

Part Three

Putting it into Practice

7 BEGINNINGS AND ENDINGS

The beginnings and endings of sermons are particularly important. They are the bridges that locate the sermon in the act of worship of which it is a part, and they are usually the sections of the sermon that are best remembered by people afterwards. Some writers on preaching recommend preparing the main body of the sermon first, and only then working on the introduction and conclusion. Others see the beginning and ending as integral to the whole plan, often suggesting that the conclusion should be the first section to be mapped out, so that the speaker is always clear where the address is leading. There is certainly much to be said for having the beginning and end written out in some detail, even if the rest of the sermon is in note form. If the start and finish are only sketchy, you can find it difficult to end the sermon in an appropriate way, and if the introduction is not fully worked, you can find yourself giving away the meat of the message before you have really started.

BEGINNINGS

In the opening two minutes, people decide whether or not they will listen to what is going to be said. The congregation may appear to be a captive audience, but their minds and affections need to be engaged, otherwise they may quickly lapse into their own daydreams. The introduction does, therefore, need to attract and keep the interest. Some preachers recommend an "attention-grabbing" opening, even one which shocks the congregation into listening. This almost certainly does not work. When people have just sat down, they need a few moments to compose themselves and to prepare for listening. The opening sentences are likely to be taken up with settling into the pew, and adapting to the voice and pattern of speaking of the preacher. Any "attention-grabbing" should probably come three or four sentences into the introduction, if at all. The other problem with trying to make a forceful opening impression is that if this level of interest is not sustained, listeners may be more likely to switch off after a short time.

One important function of the introduction is that it should act as a bridge. It should move the congregation on from what has been happening in the service up to that moment, to listening to the proclamation and interpretation of the gospel. Also, it should aim to act as a bridge between the broader context in which people live and the sermon. If there are major events taking place in the world, the nation or the local community, then raising them in the introduction will provide a realistic bridge into the sermon. Listeners are being notified that their concerns are to be addressed seriously in the context of the Christian gospel. If the introduction is based on some topical issue, then make sure it is a real question for the congregation. Opening with, "We have all been concerned this week with the importance of the election in Spain…" is unlikely to be helpful, unless it is true. Do not fall into the trap of imagining that your own concerns are shared by everyone.

Judging the length of the opening correctly is essential. An introduction which is too short and moves to the main body of the sermon quickly will not give the congregation time to find their bearings, and will leave them feeling unprepared for what is to follow. Too long a beginning, on the other hand, will make them impatient, wondering when you are going to reach the point of what you are saying. You should aim for about eight to ten sentences in the introduction, which gives people time to familiarize themselves with your voice and pattern of speaking, and provides enough space to inaugurate the main lines of thought and open up some questions.

Your opening words in the pulpit deserve some thought, and will probably need to reflect the tradition of the church in which you are preaching. In some churches, it is usual to open with a brief extempore prayer asking for God's guidance for speaker and listeners. In others, a more conventional pattern is followed, opening with either, "In the name of the Father and of the Son and of the Holy Spirit", or with, "May the words of my mouth and the thoughts of our hearts be now and always acceptable in your sight, O Lord our strength and our Redeemer". Some churches may expect their sermons to begin simply with the announcement of the text. Whatever opening you choose, it should have as its main purpose the direction of preacher and congregation towards the interpretation of the gospel. Both are engaged on a common enterprise – trying to seek God's guidance for Christian living in contemporary society.

What types of opening are available? Most introductions to sermons seem to fall into the following categories.

1. *Humour.* Some preachers try to start with a joke or a funny story, working on the assumption that the attention of the congregation will be secured. Certainly humour has its place. A group of people who laugh together immediately form a common focus. Humour as an introduction should, however, be used sparingly. It can be difficult to form a bridge between a funny story and the serious message which is to follow. Anthony de Mello's books *The Song of the Bird* and *One Minute Wisdom* both contain many short, sometimes very funny, stories which carry a Christian message and can, with care, be used as openings.
2. *Topical news.* Opening with a live topic does ensure that there is an immediate link with people in the congregation because common ground is established. Care should be taken not to be too controversial, or a large proportion may sit through the sermon feeling irritated. "We have all been overjoyed at the change of leadership in the Conservative party this week..." may win some people's attention, but it will certainly alienate others.
3. *Personal experience.* This can make an effective opening, so long as you are sufficiently aware of the danger of focusing on yourself rather than on the gospel. It is even better to refer to some experience in which the congregation has also shared – a parish social evening, the church working party, or secular preparations for a festival. These all mean that you will be on common and easily accessible ground. Do not begin with personal experience if it is likely to exaggerate your own achievements and belittle others. "As the Regius professor of divinity at Cambridge and I punted together on the river..." will only concentrate people's minds on your privileges.
4. *Stories.* Introducing a sermon by telling a story can be effective if the story is not too long and, most importantly, if it relates to the subject of the material to follow. Sometimes it can be a story from scripture, setting the reading in context. For example, a brief telling of a part of the Joseph story might introduce a sermon on a text taken from that section of Genesis.

5. *Suspense.* Openings which attempt to build up suspense, so that the listeners are waiting to find out what the topic is, rarely work well. They tend to sound contrived, and generally only serve to irritate many people. "They had lived with the problem for months. Every waking moment was occupied with worrying about it. Each new piece of information was pondered on and discussed. The appearance of every new symptom, or the disappearance of an old symptom, gave rise to despair or to hope." By now the congregation has begun to perceive that the sermon might be about some sort of illness, but they are probably exasperated at the preacher's inability to get to the point.

6. *Setting in context.* A sermon on an expository pattern might well begin by setting the context of the passage of scripture. Offering some background information about when and why 1 Corinthians was written may be a good way into a sermon on Paul's teaching about the nature of the Christian community.

7. *Questions.* Asking questions can come into many of the styles of introduction already described. Focusing on questions of real interest to the congregation is helpful, and can provide a bridge. Questions which are of no interest to most people should be avoided. "How often have you, like me, puzzled about the significance of Absalom's pillar in 1 Kings 18?" is unlikely to gain much attention.

8. *Step-downs.* Some people habitually begin sermons by gradually narrowing down the focus from a broad perspective to a single point. David Buttrick identifies this method as common in contemporary preaching, but advises against its use. Step-down has similarities with the suspense introduction because listeners do not know what this is going to be about for some time. Buttrick criticizes step-downs for having too many points of focus, leaving the congregation unsure about where they should be locating their attention. Buttrick gives the following example:

   We have all heard of the apostle Paul, a brave champion of the faith. After his astonishing conversion, he journeyed around the ancient world preaching the gospel. More than any other apostle, Paul spread good news on the earth. One of the cities Paul visited was Corinth. Corinth was a brawling seaport filled with sleazy bars, brothels and noisy bazaars, a difficult town in which to build a church. One of the problems which Paul encountered in Corinth had to do

> *with the Lord's Supper. Wealthy folk came with baskets full of food while the poor, slaves, and outcasts went hungry.*[1]

Buttrick advises that it would have been much better to have begun with a single image relating to a diverse community at the Lord's supper, because then the listeners would have been able to focus much more quickly on the core of the sermon.

ENDINGS

The end of a sermon should, like the beginning, be a bridge. It helps prepare the listeners for what is to follow in the service, particularly if a celebration of the eucharist is to follow – and it reinforces the necessity of applying what has been heard of the gospel in the sermon to ordinary life.

The following elements should be borne in mind when preparing conclusions.

1. Do not say "finally" or "in conclusion". Even worse is using both of these, or repeating either of them. You should be able to lead up to a conclusion without having to resort to such redundant phrases.
2. Do not end too abruptly. Just as a congregation needs time to settle into the opening of a sermon, so it needs time to acclimatize to the fact that the end is approaching. A gradual drawing together of threads helps to do this, as does an echo of the introduction. Briefly revisiting the main themes helps to reinforce them, but also is a useful device for signalling the end and so gives the congregation time to adjust. Ending quickly and announcing a hymn, so that everyone has to jump to their feet, does not give time for the impact of the sermon to sink in. It has become the practice in some churches to have a few minutes of silence after a sermon, which is acceptable so long as the congregation expect it. Silences which are not expected, and are of an indeterminate length, only make people think that someone has forgotten to announce what comes next.
3. Do not introduce any new material into the conclusion. The end should concentrate on drawing threads together, not on bringing in new ideas. It is, similarly, not a good idea to use illustrations or analogies in the ending, because they cannot be integrated into the main lines of thought.

4. In general terms the language of the ending should be concrete and sentences short. Both types of speaking are more easy to remember, and they are therefore more suited to the mental change of gear which takes place at the end of the sermon.

5. The conclusion should contain some recommendation or challenge for action, but this should not be vague and indeterminate. "We should all think about this a little more", is unlikely to provoke a substantial response. The best kind of ending is that with which Jesus ends many of his sayings and parables. The listeners are left with a challenge, but precisely what they must do is their own responsibility to work out.

Exercises

1. Try to recall some beginnings and endings from sermons you have heard. What made them memorable? Can you also remember the main content of these sermons?

2. Write an introduction for a Christmas sermon based on John 1.1–14, together with some notes for the main lines of development in the sermon.

Notes

1. David Buttrick, *Homiletic*, p. 93.

8 STRUCTURES

There is a craft connected with the shaping of sermons. The odd idea that preachers whose hearts have been strangely warmed will spill out sermons, instantly compelling and exquisitely formed, is, of course, nonsense. Just as a carpenter must learn to use tools in order to make a box, so preachers must acquire basic skills to preach. Though some preachers may be unusually gifted, preachers are not born, they are trained.[1]

Just as bones without flesh make a skeleton, so flesh without bones makes a jellyfish, and neither bony skeletons nor jellyfish make good sermons.[2]

Speaking to a group of people in church differs greatly from holding a one-to-one conversation with someone. Any communication with a group needs orderly arrangement if the listeners are to follow the speaker. People who would not dream of approaching a presentation in a secular setting without a carefully planned structure will, nevertheless, mount the pulpit steps having given little thought to how their message is structured. They work with the very strange idea that they can simply chat to the congregation as if they were holding an intimate conversation with a friend. While informality in the pulpit has its place, it is important to realize that communicating with a group of people requires a careful plan if the listeners are to follow what is being said. A sermon with no structure can too easily become a random collection of thoughts, or a vague ramble with no real point. It is, to use John Stott's image, a jellyfish, an unformed mass with nothing to give it shape. When preparing a sermon we need, therefore, to have a structure. This is not so that we follow it slavishly, nor so that it imposes artificially on the gospel, but so that we can communicate the essence of the subject more effectively.

Having too rigid a structure is as equally bad as having no structure. We see in a later chapter how medieval preachers were constrained by an insistence on an artificial structure, and had to force all preaching into the prescribed shape whatever the topic or the text. Some modern preachers impose upon themselves a similar affectation by attempting to be too clever. They might, for example, begin all their points with a single letter. The alliterative effect may be impressive, but the congregation is probably wondering how the preacher can force an eighth point beginning with "b" out of the material. Similarly unhelpful can be the preacher who insists on numbering each point made.

The purpose of the structure is, then, to support the sermon, but not to dominate the attention, just as the skeleton supports the body but is hidden from view. It is, however, important to recognize that no preacher can rely on a single structure and hope that it will work for all sermons. We need, rather, to have a range of different possible structures available, so that we can use them when appropriate. Ideally, each text or topic should have a structure developed specifically for it, so that the sermon becomes a working out of the internal logic of that particular subject. In reality, however, most sermons will fit into a small number of recognizable structures. Being aware of what these structures are is of considerable help to the preacher. First, this awareness will guard against the danger of always using the same sermon structure, and secondly, it gives us some possibilities to fall back on when we are struggling to prepare a sermon.

In his book *Homiletic*, David Buttrick suggests that an examination of sermon structures should not begin with the overall pattern, but with the development of the individual units of thought which make up the sermon. For Buttrick, the whole sermon is a macro structure which is comprised of a series of related micro structures. He calls these micro structures "moves". The move contains a development of a single idea, and has three elements:

1. an opening which establishes the focus of the move, and takes about three sentences;
2. the development, in which the main thought of the move is described;
3. a closure which in some way returns to the opening of the move, and again lasts for about three sentences.

According to Buttrick, moves should last about four minutes, based on the length of time a congregation can hold a single issue in its attention. Each sermon is likely to consist of four to six moves.

Buttrick develops some basic rules for moves, based on his understanding of how human consciousness works. Moves, for example:

- should contain no more than one illustration – more than one illustration per move leads to them becoming muddled with each other;
- should be capable of being expressed as a single statement;
- should have a particular focus, and should contain only one focus. Thus the move might focus on the preacher, the congregation, St Paul, on the past, the present, or the future. To mix more than one of these focuses in a move is disastrous;
- should, within a single sermon, each be shaped differently.

Buttrick gives a number of examples of "moves". The following is adapted from one of his examples to make it more accessible to British readers.

> *Make no mistake: when the Bible says "sinners", the Bible means sinners. Unvarnished, unrepentant, dyed in the wool sinners. The Bible is not talking about nice people gone astray, the good at heart prostitute or the deep down religious tax collector. No, in the Bible sinners are real sinners. Take tax collectors, for example, they were members of the Jewish Mafia, who extorted their own brothers and sisters for cash. If they walked down the streets of Jerusalem, they needed hired body guards. As for prostitutes, they were not the girl next door who had been led astray in the big city. They were street-wise, cunning, and experienced. So the sinners in the Bible were not simply good people gone astray, they were deep down sinners. And Jesus ate and drank with sinners.*[3]

It is noticeable that, in this move, Buttrick concentrates on a single thought. He introduces this thought firmly, develops it by giving specific examples, and then rounds it off with an echo of the opening. His reference to Jesus in the final sentence is the beginning of the development of a link with the next move.

OVERALL STRUCTURES

There are a great number of theoretical structures that may be used as skeletons of addresses lasting something between ten and twenty minutes. The following list is only a selection, but it contains most of the sermon structures in use in the main Christian denominations.

Obviously, a sermon may use elements from different structures – the careful implementation of variety helps to keep interest. Beware, however, of trying to mix too many structural styles in a single address – it only leads to confusion in the minds of the listeners.

Inductive and deductive sermons

These are not so much structures, but more a means of giving focus to the sermon. The inductive starts from noting seemingly haphazard things from human experience, and then moves towards a general Christian truth as the climax. For example, you might begin a Christmas sermon like this:

> *During the last few weeks of preparation for Christmas, I have noticed oases of peace among the relentless bustle. In the busy high street an old woman sat and stared at the crib outside a church. In a department store, among the noise of the electronic gadgetry and the glare of the lights, a child sat on Father Christmas's knee gazing up in trust and belief. A crowd of shoppers put down their heavy boxes and bags for a few moments to listen to the Salvation Army band playing carols. Despite the rush and the commercialism, occasionally something of the peace of Christmas breaks through.*

This opening could then be developed into a sermon which focuses on the peace brought by Christ into a relentlessly busy world.

Deductive sermons, on the other hand, begin with a general truth, and then move on to examine real human experience. The same theme of Christmas might open like this:

> *The shepherds on the hillside outside Bethlehem heard the angels sing, "Peace on earth and good will to all men". At the heart of the gospel message is the peace which is brought to us by the incarnation of the Son of God. For the gospels, peace is something much more powerful than merely the absence of war. It is to do with a quality of life offered by Jesus to those who follow him.*

This could develop into an examination of the meaning of the peace offered by Christ at Christmas and end by applying this general truth to the experience of individual people.

The shapes of inductive and deductive sermons can be shown in diagrammatic form in the following way:[4]

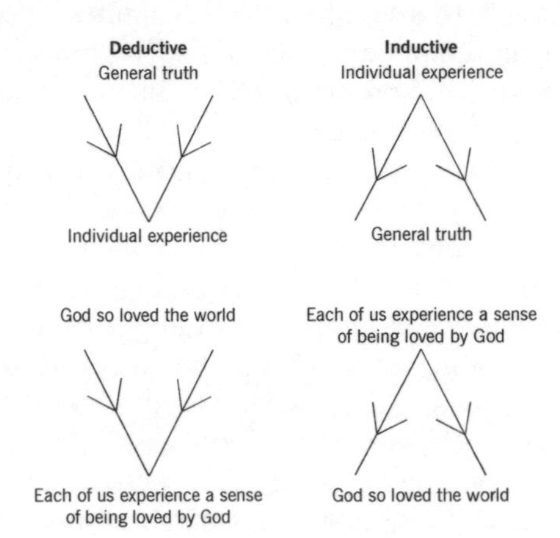

The expository sermon

This structure is especially deeply rooted in the mainstream evangelical churches. It aims to engage with the whole passage of scripture, rather than simply beginning from one or two verses. While some attention will be given to the meaning of individual verses, particularly in the early stages of the exposition, the attention is focused on the overall meaning of the passage. This is usually developed in a threefold structure:

1. an examination of the passage, especially exploring its setting in its original context, and investigating its historical meaning;
2. an interpretation of the text, offering ways it might have been understood in the past, and how it may be interpreted in the present;
3. an application of the passage to contemporary Christian life. This section is essential, and should be as fully developed as the first two. Without this, the preacher is offering an academic lecture, and not a sermon.

The story sermon

Very few preachers have a real gift for story telling. This kind of sermon can be brilliant and memorable when it works well, but dull and embarrassing when done badly. Because the Bible is largely written in narrative form, it gives limitless possibilities for those good at preaching story sermons. The great master of this style is David Kossof, and those who wish to explore the method should read some of his books.

The aim of this type of sermon is generally to help members of the congregation to put themselves into the place of participants in the story, and to be present at the events in their imaginations. The point of view from which the story is told is, therefore, important. The feeding of the five thousand, for example, could be told by the boy who brings the loaves and fishes, by one of the disciples, by a member of the crowd who is unconvinced of Jesus' messiahship, etc. The purpose of this type of sermon should be to challenge listeners to work out the implications of these events for their own lives, just as Jesus' purpose in telling parables was often to prompt his listeners into action.

Sermons which are extended analogies or parables are a variation on the narrative style of sermon. Again, they require great skill and experience, but can be highly effective. Those who hear them often remember them for years – so be careful! In *Speaking of God*, Trevor Dennis has written a fascinating collection of stories, all based on biblical themes. Here is an example of the beginning of one of these stories:

> *And God said "Let there be..." and there was, and he fell over himself in his joy. His hand flashed and a Kingfisher flew. It flashed again and another Kingfisher flew, more brightly coloured still, again and again another Kingfisher, and again and another. There was no end to them! What strange exuberance! What extravagance! What sheer delight!*
>
> *He hurled the stars into their spaces, and he knelt down to form between finger and thumb intricate, shining beetles. He danced in the river air with the mayflies and rode the great oceans on the backs of whales. He slid deep down into the very dark with strange luminous creatures that to him were not strange at all. They too came from the bright world of his imaginings. He swung from the tree with the orang-utans and rested on the seventh day with the sloths. He banistered down the swirl of the galaxy one moment and played hermit crab the next, hiding himself away with the smallest of creatures left by the tide in the rock pools.*[5]

Faceting

This is the slightly ugly name usually given to sermons which look at a single subject from a number of points of view. It is rather like holding a jewel in the hand and turning it to see the different facets it presents to the view. So, instead of trying to develop a step-by-step structure for argument, the preacher can present the topic from a series of different angles as the sermon progresses. You could, for example, prepare a sermon on baptism which describes various aspects of the sacrament:

- a channel of divine grace;
- a confession of sins;
- a mature commitment;
- initiation into the life of the community.

While these elements are clearly linked, one point does not easily progress on to another, so you develop a structure in which you consciously describe baptism from four slightly different perspectives.

The argument

In this structure, the preacher develops a particular case, leading the listeners step by step until a conclusion is reached, which is usually a challenge to adopt a particular view or act in a certain way. Those who use this structure must take great care for two reasons. First, in an argument the links between the steps are important – if these are noticeably weak then the cumulative effect fails. Secondly, this type of sermon rarely persuades people to change their views or to modify their actions. The monologue is not a good way of persuading people to change. Richard Jones in *Groundwork of Worship and Preaching* offers the following as an example outline of the sermon using an argument structure.[6]

- Everybody admits that the world is in a mess.
- But we are all dependent upon one another.
- So every individual is partly to blame.

- So you are partly responsible.
- So you must seek some source of strength and reform.
- There is only one such source – Jesus Christ.
- So you must seek reform from him.
- So you must repent, believe, and be renewed.

The quadrilateral

This structure is commonly referred to as the "Methodist quadrilateral", and is particularly suited to preaching on ethical and doctrinal topics. The plan is to consider the topic in the Bible; trace its development in Christian tradition; examine it with the use of reason; and finally locate it in contemporary Christian experience. Thus scripture, tradition, reason, and experience give the fourfold pattern. A sermon using such a structure will inevitably tend to be long – it would be difficult to do justice to any major topic in this way in less than 25 minutes. It is usual, therefore, to use it at preaching services where the sermon occupies the main focus of the worship.

There are advantages in being familiar with and practised in each of these structures; different structures will be more or less appropriate in different settings. For example, a sermon during a celebration of the Eucharist will need to be constructed in such a way as to lead the congregation on to the sacrament. It should, therefore, have an element of openness about the ending, pointing to the communion which is to follow. On the other hand, a sermon at a free church preaching service, or at an Anglican Evensong, needs to be more self-contained, because it is sharing the main focus of the service with the readings from scripture.

Secondly, familiarity with a variety of structures helps to ensure that you do not become fixed in a single way of preaching – which would be tedious for you as well as for your congregations.

Lastly, different people in congregations will be able to listen to some structures more easily than to others. Thus, the story sermon may have a lasting impact on some people while others simply miss the point. Some may prefer a step-by-step argument, but this style may strike others as dry and academic. Varying the style helps to ensure that more people can engage with the preaching.

Exercises

1. Using the readings set in your church's lectionary for next Sunday, outline three different sermon structures which you could develop.
2. Listen to some short talks on the radio – for example Alistair Cooke's *Letter from America* on Radio 4, or the talks in concert intervals on Radio 3. Briefly describe the structures used, each on no more than one sheet of paper.

Notes

1. David Buttrick, *Homiletic*, p. 37.
2. John Stott, *I Believe in Preaching*, p. 229.
3. David Buttrick, *Homiletic*, pp. 65–6.
4. *Faith and Worship*, Unit 14, p. 16.
5. Trevor Dennis, *Speaking of God*, p. 22.
6. Richard Jones, *Groundwork of Worship and Preaching*, p. 131.

9 VERBAL ILLUSTRATIONS

> *The Biblical writers knew very well that God was not literally a pregnant woman, or a tailor, or a lover, they knew very well that he did not literally bend over the first man and give him the kiss of life, or hide his glory from Moses with the palm of his hand. They knew very well what they were doing. In writing the way they did, they were not seeking to define God, or even describe him. They were dealing with metaphor, inventing images that had the mysterious power to evoke a sense of the God they encountered. They were not attempting to pin God down, like a fading butterfly in a case. They were catching at his coat tails, running after him with their bright words as he disappeared into his promised land and beyond. Their people had refused, remarkably for their day, to make a graven image of God, so they invented as many metaphors as they could, painting through their words a bewildering array of pictures, until in the gospels of the New Testament they created the most extraordinary icon of all; the image of God as a man dying on the cross.*[1]

Illustrating your sermons by using stories and analogies should not be thought of as an optional extra, but as an essential element in proclaiming the good news of the gospel. On a practical level, people remember the illustrations – every preacher has had the humbling experience of hearers remembering a story long after the main points of the sermon have been forgotten. This suggests that the stories should have their own interpretation and challenge built in. Then, if the story is remembered, the meaning will be carried with it. The story which needs explaining before its link to the message can be understood is not a good story for a sermon. Jesus' parables are the best examples of this. The story of the good Samaritan needs no explaining. You only have to tell the story and the challenge is issued.

"The medium is the message" is a piece of late twentieth-century dogma, but it has strong echoes in Christian theology. We cannot separate *what* God says from *how* he says it. The message – that through the cross and resurrection of Jesus of Nazareth we are set free – is inseparable from the medium of the message – the life and death of Jesus as proclaimed in scripture and the church. We must not, therefore, imagine that we are doing two distinct things when preaching – proclaiming the message, and then thinking of illustrations which make it more memorable and palatable.

This is why Jesus uses parables the way he does. There is a mysterious and inextricable link between his proclamation of the Kingdom of God and the world around. He does not conceive of a general religious idea, and then search for a concrete way of expressing it, but talks naturally in parables because God's Kingdom is really present in the events of the created world.

Besides the good theological reasons for making the gospel concrete, there are many practical reasons, among them being the following.

1. Verbal illustrations make listening easier. The amount of time for which a group of people can concentrate on abstract argument is strictly limited. The illustration gives them a mental rest, and allows them to hear in concrete terms what is being talked about.
2. They help ensure that sermons are remembered, and thus acted upon. Stories change lives more often than abstractions.
3. They enable the preacher to repeat points without boring and tiring the congregation. One of the difficulties of preaching is how to say the same thing a number of times without it becoming tedious.
4. Verbal illustrations make both preaching and listening more interesting.

SOURCES OF ILLUSTRATION

There are some books of sermon illustrations and stories on the market, and they have their uses. Many have been produced especially to help with school assemblies. They do, however, have their dangers. The first is that if you decide on the meat of the sermon, and then flip through a book for an illustration to tag on to it, the theme and the story will never really be parts of an integrated whole. The other danger is simply that another preacher may recently have used the same illustration with the same group of people.

There is no substitute for a fund of stories, analogies, and snippets which have been found, shaped, and saved by you. Many of the older textbooks of preaching recommended keeping a filing system of illustrations and ideas for preaching, and there are some contemporary preachers who do this. I have never been disciplined enough to make this a regular practice.

Of much more use is trying to train your mind to look for illustrations all around – there are thousands of good stories and analogies waiting to be picked up, crafted, and used. One technique which rarely fails is to read the passages of scripture on which you intend to preach at least ten days before the sermon is due, and then simply wait for illustrations. Almost every day, things will leap into your mind from the newspapers, from television, from books, from snatches of conversation overheard, from nature. By the time you sit down to prepare the sermon, you will have a whole string of ideas, and the problem then becomes what not to use.

There are some specific sources to which you need to be alert.

1. *Events in your own life.* This source needs to be treated with great care – endless personal testimonies are not useful, and there is little warrant for them in the biblical material. But often the personal story, observation, or thought can be used effectively. One preacher was well known for always basing his sermon after his summer holiday on some event which had occurred, and people eagerly awaited it, and remembered it.

2. *Newspapers and television.* A vast fund of illustrations is available. Science, art, "human interest" stories, and politics all provide material. There is the added advantage that many of your listeners will be familiar with the same material, and so you begin on common ground.

3. *The workplace.*

   Crewe comes to mind and its great railway works: immense locomotives swinging off the ground while men continued to work on them; the crane under the roof, which, at an "upward glance", seemed to bring whatever men needed. I remember the manufacture of rails, signal boxes, and all the impedimenta of a vast transport system. I remember also the three skilful craftsmen working quietly in their own department on artificial limbs.

   "Isn't that a good hand, sir? Look, the fingers move! With a glove on, it would look quite normal." I turned that to good use. The guide had said on the early part of my tour:

"We have a railway system as near to perfect, I think, as any that has been devised..."

Really?

Yet those craftsmen, serving one company only, were working all day and every day on artificial limbs.[2]

Illustrative openings to two of my own sermons follow. Each of them is based on an event which happened while on holiday, and each of them uses something that will be familiar to most people. The first illustration is rather complex, because it weaves together a real-life image, and a fragment of a poem which was brought to mind by the event. It does, however, provide a wealth of leads into a sermon on the place of the Christian faith in a secular world, and the nature of mission.

Matthew 4.12–20 "As he was walking by the Sea of Galilee..."

This summer I went to the west coast of France for my holiday. Standing ankle-deep in the Atlantic Ocean as the tide retreated, I felt the water dragging at my feet. Sand was pulled from under me; shingle was sucked out to sea. The force of the outgoing tide almost made me overbalance. As the ocean noisily withdrew, I was reminded of a line in Matthew Arnold's poem Dover Beach. *Returning home, I turned up the poem, part of which runs as follows:*

> *The sea of faith*
> *Was once, too, at the full, and round earth's shore*
> *Lay like the folds of a bright girdle furl'd;*
> *But now I only hear*
> *Its melancholy, long, withdrawing roar,*
> *Retreating to the breath*
> *Of the night-wind down the vast edges drear*
> *And naked shingles of the world.*

We live our Christian lives in a world from which the tide of faith seems to have withdrawn. How do we react? Arnold's lament at the passing of the full tide of religious faith was reflected by my son. He enjoys surfing, and for him the outgoing tide meant no more fun. He sat on the beach and grumbled, asking when he could surf again. My answer was, of course, that soon the tide would turn and before long he could indulge in his sport. But for my daughter, low tide revealed a delightful new world. Among the rocks were crabs, sea anemones, star fish, and many other delights. She was happy in the new world which had come into being and spent many hours discovering its wonders. The reactions of my two children to low tide were for me a parable of how Christians view today's world.

Do we react to twentieth-century secular society by waiting for the turn of the tide? Do we bemoan the fact that the Church and the faith no longer hold the position of prominence which they enjoyed in the past, and look for a revival of a former age, a return to the time when all believed? Or, should we recognize that the new world revealed by the retreating tide is just as full of God's glory and presence as was the old world in which faith played a more overtly prominent part? Human beings in today's world are no longer the naturally religious animals they once were. No longer is everything understood in terms of divine control and intervention. Should we not, therefore, dispense with the attempt to impose faith upon people and accept the Christian faith as a private world-view equally valid with all other world views?

My second illustration was originally an experience looking for a sermon. As the event happened, I was conscious that it had preaching possibilities, and so stored it at the back of my mind while I awaited an opportunity to use it.

While on holiday in Cornwall, we spent a day at a theme park. Every time we take the children to one of these places – about once a year – I feel a little older. Part of this park was a science exploratory – a hands-on series of experiments and experiences meant to stimulate the child, and I suppose the adult, into understanding basic scientific principles. Inside the exploratory was a small triangular room, large enough for only one person, with its walls covered with mirrors. I was fascinated. I could see myself from the side. I could see the back of my head from various angles. As I slowly moved, so did the image of me. I caught glimpses of myself I had never seen before, and it gradually dawned on me that I was seeing myself as others see me.

The queue of children outside the room was building up, but no matter – I intended to get my money's worth, and besides, I felt a sermon coming on. I realized what a privilege it was to see myself as family, friends, colleagues see me. I was not sure that I liked catching glimpses of myself unawares. I am used to seeing myself straight on in the mirror, while I shave or comb my hair. Otherwise, I am not much given to self-contemplation.

Hang on, I thought – the kids outside were getting ever more restless – if it's exciting to see myself as other people see me, how about if I could see myself as God sees me? What if I could catch myself unawares not just on the outside, but on the inside as well? The unattended moment, as Eliot describes it, when I unexpectedly see myself and God for real, afresh, with new insight.

By now, there was a near riot outside this room of mirrors, so I had to get out, but for the rest of the holiday I was trying to imagine how I looked, how I seemed, how I appeared to others and to God. What I was searching for was a perspective, a point of view from which to observe.

Exercises

1. What illustrations from sermons you have heard can you remember? Can you also remember the main points of the sermons?
2. Suggest other sources of illustration, in addition to those described above.
3. Suggest some possible illustrations you have come across this week for sermons, in the news, in the events of your life, in reading, etc.

DEVELOPING ILLUSTRATIONS

Each of the illustrations listed above needed considerable polishing before reaching its present form. A good idea for an illustration is only the starting point – you then need to work at it so that it is interesting and conveys the message at which you are aiming. The length of illustrations is often disregarded, but a good initial idea can be ruined by the way it is developed.

Exercise

Two illustrations follow. The first is part of a Christmas Day sermon, and is much too long. Taking about 10 minutes, try to reduce this illustration to about 180 words, without allowing it to lose its impact.

The second illustration, part of an Easter sermon, is too short. Again, taking about 10 minutes, develop it into an image with more impact.[3]

Illustration A

Lots of people are bored in church because nothing seems to happen, I expect you feel like that sometimes. Anyway, people who say not enough happens in church would have been even more critical in the Middle Ages. Then, in the great churches and cathedrals, you know the sorts of places you wander around on holiday, full of loud-talking Americans with their cameras and videos. In these churches and cathedrals everything went on behind the big wooden rood screens, which as you can still see in many places today, divide the interior of the church. Services were conducted by the priests, all dressed up in their finery, and the sacraments were celebrated behind the screen while the ordinary people like you and me had to stand around in the main body of the church. They couldn't see a thing and they probably chatted most of the time, just like many people do now before the service.

Anyway, at some stage in the Middle Ages, members of the craft guilds like shoemakers and silversmiths decided to take that which was holy and shut up in church out into the streets for all the common people. They set up stages on wagons and then re-enacted Bible stories, from Adam to Revelation, where the people were. I expect it was a great laugh for most of the population, you know the sort of people who are glued to their television sets for *Eastenders* and *Coronation Street*.

So the people were now part of the action, involved in the salvation story, and they were not cut off by the rood screen. They saw the nativity story, the trial, and the crucifixion, acted out before their eyes. That which had been hidden, the presence of God himself, was revealed to all.

"The Word was made flesh and dwelt among us." The point of this story is that at Christmas, God took away the rood screen, so that we can see what he is like and what was going on.

Illustration B

In some parts of the country, gardeners plant their potatoes on Good Friday. They are buried with Christ so that they might rise again. We have symbols of resurrection all around us.

Notes

1. Trevor Dennis, *Speaking of God*, p. 3.
2. William E. Sangster, *The Craft of Sermon Illustration*, pp. 59–60.
3. This exercise is taken from *Faith and Worship*, Unit 14, p. 20.

10 USING YOUR VOICE IN PREACHING

Your voice is a very particular expression of your own personality, for it is the means by which you convey your thoughts and feelings in an immediate way to other people – it is how you reach out to them, so you require it to do justice to what you want it to communicate. What is important here is that it is the outward expression of your inner self, it is the means by which people understand and get an impression of you.[1]

However thorough your reading and preparation, however inspired by the Spirit, however brilliant a script you may have written, it is all worthless unless you can be heard. The most common complaint from members of congregations is not that they were unable to understand the sermon, or that they disagreed with the doctrines being propounded, but that they could not hear.

Remember that those who are hard of hearing generally sit near the back of the church. It can be infuriating, especially for the preacher at an evening service with twenty people present, to find that they are all sitting in the back row. This may happen for a number of reasons, but I have two favourite theories. The first is that where people sit, especially in Anglican churches, is still determined by the ancient practice of pew rents. The annual rent for the pew at the front of the church was perhaps five guineas, and it was occupied by the local land owner. Further back in the church, the rental decreased and so the seats would be occupied by those further down the social scale. At the back the pews were free, and were occupied by servants. Thus the seating in church reflected the social structure of the community. Deep in the English folk memory is the feeling that sitting near the front of the church is proclaiming yourself to be near the top of the social ladder, and many people, especially the older generation, feel uncomfortable with this.

The other possible reason for people always sitting in the same place is even more deeply rooted. I asked a woman in her nineties why she always sat where she did. She replied that she and her husband had always sat together in that pew. He had died over twenty years earlier, but she felt closer to him sitting there in church than at any other time in the week. Clearly to force her to move would have been very insensitive, and would almost certainly have meant that she was not able to listen to or participate properly in the worship.

Recognizing some of the common faults in the way preachers use their voices may help us to avoid making the same mistakes. Try to think of preachers you have known who are prone to these problems.

- Speaking at a single speed, usually too quickly, so that the words become a blur. Occasionally the preacher speaks with an exaggerated slowness, which is equally difficult to listen to.
- Preaching with the special "pulpit" voice. This can be particularly irritating, and the congregation will wonder why a special religious intonation is needed when preaching or leading worship. It implicitly suggests that religion is divorced from what goes on outside church, because a special way of speaking needs to be adopted in worship.
- Speaking too quietly is common, even among experienced preachers. In your early days as a preacher, it is almost certain that if you feel you are speaking too slowly and too loudly you probably have it about right.
- Too much volume is as difficult to listen to as too little. Words become distorted and, just as important, the preacher's voice soon becomes strained.
- Sudden changes in volume are difficult to listen to. There should be a variety of volume, but to switch from a whisper to a yell can be disconcerting for the listeners. There are better methods of keeping a congregation awake than periodically shouting at them.
- Consonants, especially t's and d's, are often missed off words. Some accents are especially liable to this. Equally difficult to listen to is the practice of laying stress on final t's and d's in words – it can sound very artificial.
- Dropping the voice at the end of the sentence frequently happens, with the result that the last one or two words are lost.

> ***Exercise***
>
> From the pulpit, tell a short story based on notes you have made in advance. Ask three or four friends or colleagues to note any of the above problems they detect in your voice. Do not be too sensitive about this – accept their advice graciously.

There are some simple precautions which can be taken to help ensure that you are heard.

- Keep your head up when preaching. If you are buried in your notes, your voice cannot carry.
- Look at members of the congregation (but not too long at any individual or you will embarrass them). You will subconsciously adjust your voice so that you can be heard by those you are looking at.
- Imagine you are speaking to someone in the back row.
- Open your mouth a little wider than usual. At first this will feel strange, but you will soon do it automatically.
- Listen carefully to other public speakers, especially those you think are particularly good. Notice how they use speed and pitch to convey meaning. Try to practise their good points yourself.
- Use pauses intelligently. They can be a useful means of stressing important points, as they act like punctuation in written communication. Pause before moving from one subject to another. Do not, however, use pauses over-dramatically. Remember, pauses always seem longer to the speaker than to the listener.

USING A MICROPHONE

Even now, many preachers will encounter a public address system only infrequently. Do not be frightened – it is there to help you, and you should let it work for you. There are two basic types of microphones in use in churches: those which are fixed to the pulpit or lectern; and those which are clipped on to the preacher's clothing (usually called "radio mikes").

With both types, ensure that you are familiar with how to switch the equipment on and off if you need to.

Fixed microphones are usually directional. You must speak towards them, but not too closely into them, as this can distort your voice. Avoid moving your head from side to side, or backwards and forwards, as this will cause your voice to sound alternately soft and loud.

Radio microphones are usually very sensitive. They are clipped on or near the jacket lapel, and have a small aerial and box attached by wire which usually slips into your pocket. An on/off switch is located on the box. Make sure you can operate the switch easily, and only switch on when you want to speak – if you leave it on during hymns, the congregation will hear your amplified voice soaring above everyone else. Be careful, also, that you do not leave the microphone switched on while you are in the vestry. It has been known for gossip between people in the vestry to be broadcast throughout the church. One unfortunate preacher even went to the lavatory while his microphone was live and broadcasting to the whole church.

Exercises

1. If your own church does not have a public address system make a point of going somewhere that does, and ask if you can practise with the equipment.
2. Ask someone to tape-record you while speaking in public – even a small group setting is useful. If you have not heard your own voice before, this can be a disconcerting experience. This is because we hear most of our own voice through the bones of the skull, not through the ears. Listen to the tape and note down ways in which you think you could improve.

HOW IS THE VOICE PRODUCED?

Each person's voice is distinctive, and its production depends on a unique conjunction of factors. Each of the following has an effect.

1. Your environment is important. Throughout life, everyone hears other people speak, and so they adapt their own voices unconsciously. This obviously has an effect on the accent with which one speaks. Different regional accents are to be welcomed – Jesus and his followers spoke with a rough north-country Galilean accent – and they do not detract from clarity if used well. The voice is also affected by the wider environment. We only need to reflect that country accents tend to be slow and musical, while urban accents are quick and flat, to realize how important the environment is.
2. The voice is affected by how the individual perceives sound. Some people listen accurately and perceive a wide variety of sounds which they can easily reproduce. Others are less accurate in their perception of sound, and thus in their sound production.
3. The speaker's physiological make-up is vital. The muscles of the face, throat, and chest all have an effect. In general a large person can produce more volume with less effort, but this is not always the case.
4. Degrees of nervousness have their effect on the voice. When a preacher feels inhibited or ill at ease, the breathing becomes more shallow, and the voice sounds less substantial, becoming high and thin.
5. The most essential element in voice production is breath control. Good breathing is the key to a good voice, for it controls volume, tone, and pace. An excellent way of improving breathing and developing the voice is singing – a form of exercise to which preachers generally have easy access.

All these elements affect all preachers, and we must use the resources available to our voices rather than fighting against them and trying to change them too drastically. We cannot stop ourselves from being nervous – some feeling of apprehension is probably a good thing when we climb the pulpit steps – but some knowledge of how the voice works can help us to control the way the nervousness affects our speaking. The exercises below should be practised every day for a week, and then can be used before speaking in public.

Do not, however, become too conscious of the technical production of your voice. You sound at your best when the technicalities are forgotten, and you speak instinctively.

Exercises for developing the breathing and voice control

1. Lie on your back on the floor and consciously relax your muscles, especially the ribs and the diaphragm. Concentrate on keeping the neck and shoulders free. Speak some line of text that you know – for example a passage from the Bible, or a poem, or some Shakespeare. Begin quietly, and gradually increase the volume as you go on, but take care that you keep it keyed to the same pitch.
2. Stand up and start speaking the text with your hands behind your head to open the ribs. As you go on, gradually bring the arms down.
3. Sing part of your text quite loudly on one note, making the breath last to the end of the phrase. Then speak some of it, being conscious of your breath supporting the sound.
4. Shout two or three lines of text, taking care not to tense your neck, then speak the rest, always feeling the extra energy from the centre of your diaphragm.
5. Jog heavily around the room or on one spot, imagining a great weight on you as you jog. Speak while you are doing this, gradually increasing the volume without letting the pitch rise.
6. Speak while lying on the floor, checking regularly to see there is no tension in the neck. Use the floor as a sounding board and feel the vibrations in your chest.
7. Lie on the floor on your front, with your head turned to one side. Hum in this position and feel the vibrations on the floor. Also speak and sing some text while lying in this position.
8. Standing, do the same as the last exercise, but humming and speaking into a corner so that the walls bounce back some of the sound. If you have a piano, speak down into the body of it, where the strings are, with the sustaining pedal on. You will hear the vibrations coming back at you, which will help you to increase your own.
9. Sing a piece of text like an operatic recitative, making up your own tune as you go along. Then speak it normally.[2]

Notes

1. Cicily Berry, *Your Voice and How to use it Successfully* (Virgin, 1990), p. 9.
2. Exercises adapted from *Your Voice and How to use it Successfully*.

11 THE PREACHER'S ENVIRONMENT

Not only is your voice important, of almost equal significance is the environment within which people will listen to your sermons – and remember that as the preacher, you yourself are part of that environment. In this chapter we consider three elements of the environment that have an impact upon the sermon.

THE BUILDING

It is difficult to stand in a pulpit you have never entered before and preach in a building in which you have never spoken before. You should, therefore, develop a strategy for getting to know the building before you begin the sermon. If preaching in a church which is strange to you, make a point of arriving early. Stand in the church for a few moments, and look around, feeling the atmosphere. Sit in a pew, and try to imagine what it is like to be a worshipper there. Look up to the pulpit, and picture seeing and listening to yourself. If you have time, speak a few sentences from the pulpit and ask someone at the back of the church to comment on your audibility. If you are not leading the whole of the service, it is good practice at least to read one of the lessons yourself before you begin to preach, so that you become familiar with the acoustics of the building, and the congregation begin to tune in to your voice.

Every building has different acoustics. Any large building will have "dead spots" which are more difficult to reach. Stone – the material from which many churches are constructed – is especially bad for audibility. It tends to magnify the vowels and kill the consonants. In most churches there is usually one place to which you can speak in order to achieve the best overall results, but you can only find out where this place is by experimenting. The problem is magnified by the fact that different voices produce different results in the same building.

Exercise

Visit a number of churches with your group or with some friends. In each of them sit in a pew, and feel the atmosphere of the building. Then stand in the pulpit, read a Bible passage, and speak for three or four minutes. Ask your colleagues to comment on how your voice responds in the different settings. Make some notes on how you felt in each building, and compare them with notes made by your colleagues.

DISTRACTIONS

> *Please listen to me – you are not paying attention. I am talking to you about the Holy Scriptures, and you are looking at the lamps and the people lighting them. It is very frivolous to be more interested in what the lamp lighters are doing. After all, I am lighting a lamp too – the lamp of God's word.*[1]

If you are preaching as a visitor, there is probably nothing you can do about most of the distractions found in the building. You may, however, be preaching regularly in the same church, and you might be able to bring about some changes.

Some members of the congregation will be easily distracted; others will concentrate on what is being said despite what is going on around them. It does, however, make good sense to try to limit the distractions. The following elements commonly detract from the sermon.

- *Temperature*. It is not usual for churches to be too warm, except perhaps some modern buildings with glass walls in the summer. Generally, the problem is low temperatures. Listening to a sermon with cold feet can be very difficult. If there is a heating system, make sure that it is switched on well before the service.

- *Noisy heating systems*. The noise of fans or pumps can make it impossible for people to hear you speak. The best solution is to switch them off, at least for the duration of the sermon, but if it then becomes too cold the distraction is just as great.

- *Clocks*. Few churches have a clock fitted internally, but in those which do, the knowledge that the congregation can count the minutes ticking away as you preach is not comforting. In some churches the bells chime the hour and the quarters, and this can prove disturbing. Ancient churches commonly had a sand-filled hour glass fixed near to the pulpit, so that preacher and people could see the allotted time for the sermon slipping away. It was not unknown for the preacher to come to the end of the sand and then turn the instrument over for it to start again!
- *Poor public address systems*. If the microphone is causing hisses and crackles, and it is making you difficult to listen to – switch it off.
- *Children*. Obviously one would not suggest that children should not be present in church, but a screaming child negates all the work you have put into the sermon by guaranteeing that no one hears. Some churches have "surprise bags" – a small bag of (quiet!) toys and colouring materials – which are given to those with children on the way in. These can prove very effective, but there are other methods of keeping children quiet. When our daughter was very small she could be noisy in church, and my wife usually took two biscuits to the service and produced them at the beginning of the sermon. Each biscuit lasted six or seven minutes, so she was quiet for the average length of the morning sermon. If the two biscuits were finished before the sermon ended, she would demand another one loudly. For some time it was the tradition in the family to judge the length of the sermon in terms of the number of biscuits Rachel could eat. A long sermon was "three biscuits"; we once had a visiting preacher who went on for five biscuits!

However firm your efforts to minimize distractions, some people will always become bored and stop listening. They will count the organ pipes, think about dinner, mentally criticize other people's clothes, drop hymn books… the list is endless. If you are alert you will soon learn to spot when you have lost the interest of the majority of the congregation.

Exercise

Take a notebook with you next time you attend a service, and jot down the potential distractions in the building. What strategies could you use to counter some of these?

THE PREACHER AS PART OF THE ENVIRONMENT

We went to church for the morning service, and heard a sermon which suggested some reflections. The preacher appeared to be on the verge of middle age; he may well have another quarter of a century of active ministry before him. What kind of preacher will he have become by the time his course is run? He must deteriorate, for we all do that as we decline into old age; but how pitifully small will be his stock of thought and knowledge which will have been running out without replenishment on the way! Mannerisms such as his may soon develop into incapacitating and ineradicable faults. Surely a little modesty, a little industry, a little effort could have corrected them; but, most probably, these are now, in his own view, distinctive excellencies. He is rather proud of them than otherwise![2]

As preachers, we are in church to point people to God, and not to draw attention to ourselves. There is the real possibility of conflict here. The medium through which the gospel is proclaimed is the preacher, so the preacher's personality, gestures, and dress all have an effect on the message. The dangers are that if the preacher is too strong and memorable as an individual, the congregation will go away with firm impressions of the preacher and may remember little of the message. If, on the other hand, the personality of the preacher comes across as weak, then the listeners may gain the impression that the message also is weak. Consider the following three factors.

- *Posture*. Aim for a natural, unselfconscious dignity. Stand upright and relaxed. Slouching in the pulpit produces the impression that the sermon is casual and unimportant. Standing to rigid attention puts both the preacher and the congregation on edge. Not only does a relaxed but upright posture look best, but it also aids good voice production.

- *Gestures*. The use of the hands and of a range of facial expression helps give meaning to your words, and are natural expressions of your personality. Do not stand like a statue or the sermon will seem dull and lifeless, no matter how exciting its content. You should, however, use gestures sparingly. The same movement of the hand or the same smile repeated a dozen times soon robs the sermon of a sense of spontaneity. Spend some time practising your gestures in front of a mirror, and experimenting with portraying different emotions with your hands and face.
- *Dress*. The preacher's dress can be a sensitive issue – remember that the main purpose is to help people to worship and not to irritate them. Different modes of dress will be appropriate on different occasions. For an outdoor rally or a family service, casual dress may be right. For a formal occasion in a traditional church it is probably best to wear the accustomed robes or gown.

Exercise

Make some notes about the positive and negative aspects of the posture, gestures, and dress of preachers you have heard recently.

Notes

1. Chrysostom (347–407), quoted in Jay Adams, *Consumers Guide to Preaching*, p. 81.
2. From Hensley Henson, *Retrospect of an Unimportant Life*, 1945.

12 SOME PRACTICAL MATTERS

As your experience as a preacher grows, so the little practicalities associated with sermons become second nature. Initially, however, these need some thought, and you need to be on the lookout for traps into which you might unintentionally fall. Some of the suggestions in this chapter might seem obvious and simple, but I have seen people tripped up by all of them, and have even stumbled on some myself.

You need to give some consideration to the paper on which you write your sermon or notes. If, for example, you write on A4 paper, there is the danger that the top of the sheet will flop over the pulpit, making it not only difficult to read but also distracting for listeners. A5, or A4 folded, is better. Write legibly; it is embarrassing to find words you cannot read in your own script. Some people use files with slip-in pockets which are readily obtainable in stationers. The advantage of these is that if you need to preach without a pulpit, they make the notes much more manageable and ensure that they are kept in the correct order.

If you are not familiar with the church in which you are preaching, go up into the pulpit before the service begins. I heard recently of a preacher who took the wrong route from his seat to the pulpit and found himself in a dead end of pews. The congregation will find it difficult to take your sermon seriously if you get lost in the church. On climbing the steps, notice whether you are likely to trip. Once in the pulpit check that the height of the reading desk is right for you, and adjust it if it is adjustable. Make sure you know how to switch on the light if there is one, and how the microphone works.

Before the service, check that all the pages of your notes are together. Turning over a page and finding that you have left your last three sheets in the vestry is a not uncommon experience.

It is a good practice to get into the habit of putting your notes into the pulpit before the service. This ensures that you have found your way to the place you will preach from, and that you have your notes. It also means that you do not leave your notes in the vestry, or on the seat at which you are sitting during the service. If you need a Bible to refer to while preaching, make sure that there is one in the pulpit and that it is of a suitable size for you to read. It might help to mark any places you intend to refer to.

You might wish to keep a discreet eye on the time while you are preaching. Rather than openly looking at a wristwatch regularly, it is better to slip your watch off and put it on the edge of the pulpit (out of sight of the congregation) before you begin preaching.

Make sure that the Bible readings you expect are those which are actually being read. It can be very difficult if you have prepared a sermon on one text and someone reads an entirely different passage. If this happens, the temptation is to be cross with the reader at the beginning of the sermon.

Make sure that you know exactly when in the service the sermon is to take place. Also, be aware of what is to happen immediately after the sermon. If there is a hymn, for example, are you expected to announce it? Ensure that you have a note of the hymn number in the pulpit with you in case you cannot see the hymn board from where you are standing.

What should you do with sermon notes after you have preached from them? Some people immediately consign them to the wastepaper basket, insisting that they never preach the same sermon twice. Some keep all their sermons, while others retain only those which they consider to be worth repeating. While it is rare to find a preacher who will admit to preaching the same sermon frequently, many say that they will rework an old sermon for a new occasion. It is therefore possible for a sermon to improve over a period of time, and it can be instructive to compare your own work as it develops. If you do keep sermons, be sure to mark them with the date and place in which they were preached, and also with the biblical text on which they were based. Many preachers develop a filing system for their sermons, classifying them by subject, text or season of the church's year.

These practical points may sound elementary, but they are nevertheless important. After preaching for some time, the experienced preacher will do most of these things unconsciously, but it is worth while giving some attention to them, especially in the early stages of preaching.

Part Four

Sermons for Different Occasions

13 MORAL AND SOCIAL TOPICS

Our task as preachers is neither to avoid all areas of controversy, nor to supply slick answers to complex questions in order to save people the bother of thinking. Either way is to treat them like children who are unable to think for themselves, and to condemn them to perpetual immaturity. Instead, it is our responsibility to teach them with clarity and conviction the plain truths of scripture, in order to help them develop a Christian mind, and to encourage them to think with it about the great problems of the day, and so to grow into maturity in Christ.[1]

The obvious question to raise at the outset is whether we should preach sermons on ethical and social subjects at all. Many Christians would argue that if a person is living the new life of the gospel then their moral conduct will be correct. Beyond that, we have no mandate for preaching on moral, social, or political issues which are not directly addressed in scripture. The view that politics should not be preached from the pulpit is often used to deny the right of preachers to comment on contemporary moral issues which have political implications.

Other people may suggest that preachers are not necessarily experts on the whole range of moral and social issues, which is undoubtedly true. There is certainly weight in the position which asserts that the sermon is a far from ideal vehicle for addressing complex moral issues and teasing out their implications, and that preaching on them tends to lead to over-simplification. Also to be borne in mind is the fact that, on most contentious moral and social issues, Christians can and do hold very different views with integrity.

There is, however, a long tradition of giving moral guidance in the sermon, and of issuing challenges to the social and political status quo. All Christians are aware that the gospel has ethical implications, and it is undeniable that in the Bible there is clear ethical instruction. This is given not only in the personal sphere, but it also impinges on relationships within the home, where the reciprocal duties of husbands and wives, parents and children, and masters and slaves are clearly related to the relationship between Christ and the Church (Ephesians 5.21—6.9; 1 Peter 2.18—3.7).

Beyond personal and domestic relationships, wider social questions are addressed in the prophetic literature and in the gospels. The teaching about non-retaliation and loving one's enemies in the Sermon on the Mount (Matthew 5.38–48 and Luke 6.27–36) opens up our minds to the realization that Jesus' message extends into all human relationships – including relationships with those one does not find it easy to get on with.

John Stott helpfully describes a series of concentric circles, "beginning with personal ethics, then moving on through the churchly, the domestic and the social to issues which have a political dimension".[2] All these circles are the business of the preacher, for the good news of Jesus extends to all areas of human life and to all human relationships. As David Buttrick puts it, "If Jesus Christ is only a personal saviour, who is going to save us from the 'Powers and Principalities' in the social world?"[3]

We cannot assume that silence from the pulpit implies neutrality on ethical matters. It is much more likely to be received as tacit acceptance by congregations. If such issues as experimentation on human foetuses, Sunday trading, homelessness, changing sexual morality, and gaps between rich and poor, are simply not mentioned in sermons, then our hearers will probably assume either that these things are not relevant to the Christian gospel or that the preacher is happy to accept the contemporary state of morality.

Preachers, then, have a duty to address ethical questions in sermons. The danger of over-simplification is, however, real. To imply that there is a single, correct Christian view on any of the complex topics mentioned above is clearly false. Christians of firm conviction, equally rooted in scripture and in the church's tradition, can and do hold very different positions on these questions. This should not, however, prevent us from addressing these topics, for people in congregations are struggling to apply the gospel to contemporary life. Our duty as preachers is to offer them some guidance in this struggle.

Perhaps even more dangerous is the tendency of preachers to pass off their own opinions as the only Christian view. They may bring into the sermon their own half thought out views and their own misunderstandings about the facts of the topic. We need some method of thinking through an ethical question as we prepare to preach about it. If we are able to use such a method, we will be offering to the congregation a way of dealing with a moral subject within the context of Christian teaching, and this will become a model for them when they need to do their own ethical thinking.

From these thoughts, a number of points arise which need to be kept in mind when preaching on ethical and social subjects. They are not a series of steps to be worked through, but some principles upon which this type of sermon needs to be built.

1. How do you decide what ethical topics to address? The simple answer is that you do not have to go looking for topics – rather they will present themselves to you. Live issues fill the media, and many of them cry out to be commented on in the light of the gospel. If you are working with subjects which catch the interest of your hearers, you will not need to struggle to gain their attention. But you must make sure that you are concerned with real issues. Nothing is more conducive to boredom than the preacher addressing questions about which no one is concerned.

2. Be sure to find out the facts. Preaching from one's own poor grasp of a subject is unlikely to help the congregation. The preacher should, therefore, read quality newspapers and books on current ethical and political topics. Just as important, if there is a member of the congregation who has knowledge and experience of the topic, then talk to them. There may be a medical practitioner, a social worker, or a politician among the church's members. Spending some time with them and finding out the facts sends two important messages to the congregation. First it shows that you value their expertise, and secondly it demonstrates the important principle that in Christian ethics taking trouble to understand the relevant information must be the first step. All moral theology must be based firmly on an appreciation of the facts, otherwise we cannot know what issues we should be applying scripture and Christian tradition to. We can only begin to formulate the questions we wish to put to the gospel when we have an appropriate grasp of the situation.

3. We must recognize that preaching on ethical and social issues will probably demand a different type of structure from sermons which begin with a biblical text. The ethical sermon begins from a dilemma in real life, and seeks to apply Christian

insights. So, rather than beginning with a text and attempting to work out how it impinges on the Christian life, here we are beginning from a burning issue and seeking a Christian response. The preacher quickly learns that simply quoting biblical texts is no easy way to solve ethical dilemmas. We are seeking to explore how ethical thinking and decision making can take place within the overall themes of scripture. Setting the problem within the revelatory pattern of creation, fall, redemption, and consummation is much more demanding than finding some verses in a concordance. The preacher who manages to explore the topic within the Christian scheme is, however, helping the congregation to develop a way of seeing all contemporary issues in the light of the gospel.

4. The preacher must appreciate the congregation's needs and presuppositions. It is disastrous to assume that the congregation is a blank sheet of paper waiting to be written on by the preacher. It will almost certainly be the case that in the congregation are individuals who have more insight into a particular moral or social topic than the preacher, either through personal experience or professional knowledge. But, experts aside, most members read the newspapers and watch television. They, too, will approach the subject with opinions which are more or less strongly held. The preacher must find a way of acknowledging these opinions without necessarily endorsing them. This becomes particularly sensitive when the topic has political implications, for the preacher and the congregation may both have assumptions that have nothing to do with the Christian gospel but which deeply colour their ethical decision making.

5. On most ethical subjects there is a valid contribution to be made by disciplines other than theology. When we are trying to understand how individuals relate to one another and how societies operate, it is legitimate to use the insights of psychology, sociology, and economics. Of course, these must be used with care, firstly because the preacher is unlikely to have specialized expertise in these areas, but also because a psychological or sociological analysis of a problem does not necessarily lead to answer. It may well point to sharp questions to be asked; we shall then need to work hard at applying Christian insights before the material begins to take on the characteristics of a sermon.

6. The preacher should acknowledge that there may be no distinctive Christian viewpoint on the subject and should be open about this in the sermon. For example, there are good arguments in favour of and against both capitalist and socialist economic systems, but neither system is clearly endorsed in scripture. To imply that either system is more true to the gospel is a travesty, for none of our contemporary economic systems was envisaged by the biblical writers. The preacher should, therefore, be willing to let the congregation hear that it is legitimate to struggle with ethical and social questions, and perhaps to remain open about the conclusions. If we speak openly about our struggle, then members of the congregation will feel more positive about acknowledging their own dilemmas and uncertainties. This stance would also emphasize that Christians may legitimately disagree with one another about major ethical issues.

Exercise

1. What current ethical and social issues do you think it would be appropriate to preach about?
2. Choose one of these issues and make a list of the information you would need about the topic before you could begin to construct a sermon.
3. What biblical material might you be able to use in your thinking about this topic?

Notes

1. John Stott, *I Believe in Preaching*, p. 173.
2. *I Believe in Preaching*, p. 155.
3. David Buttrick, *Homiletic*, p. 421.

14 PREACHING ON SPECIAL OCCASIONS

Almost all churches have services which are seen as highlights within the calendar. The major Christian festivals of Easter and Christmas; the "folk-religion" festivals of Harvest and Mothering Sunday; national occasions such as Remembrance Day; and local events such as a civic service or a school founders' day. Some preachers regard such special occasions as tedious, and become irritated with people who only attend church for these events. It is much better to treat them as opportunities for explaining the gospel to those who rarely hear it. For regular worshippers, special occasions should not be regarded as interruptions to the normal Sunday pattern, but as genuine highlights which bring into a clearer focus certain aspects of the Christian message and the church's life.

It is tempting to say that preaching on special occasions is no different from preaching to the regular congregation on an ordinary Sunday. There are, however, some significant differences which must be taken into consideration, and which apply to almost all special occasions:

- there are usually more people in church on special occasions;
- there are often more children than usual, especially at services for Christmas, Mothering Sunday and Harvest;
- there is a greater proportion of occasional churchgoers;
- the congregation will have certain clear expectations that the worship and sermon will address the theme of the occasion they have come to celebrate.

Before looking in detail at the different types of special occasion which occur in most churches, there are some general guidelines that may be outlined.

- Do not grumble at people who have come only for the special occasions but do not attend regularly. This tactic annoys everyone in the congregation.

- Do not exclude the occasionals. Give the impression that it is a real pleasure to have them joining in worship.
- Concentrate on preaching the basic Christian message – some people present may not have heard it before.
- If the choir or a section of the congregation has prepared a special item, be sure to refer to it positively in the sermon.
- People have come to church on this occasion for a particular reason – use this fact in your sermon.

While all special occasions share most of the characteristics described above, there are differences, and each has its own flavour. These occasions can be grouped under four headings, each of which share some features.

MAJOR CHRISTIAN FESTIVALS

People still attend church in very large numbers at Christmas, although the other major Christian festivals of Easter, Pentecost, and Advent are less well supported. However, these festivals, together with Lent and Holy Week, Ascension and some churches' patronal festivals, do have significantly large numbers of occasional worshippers.

The group of people generally described as "the fringe" differs from church to church. In a lively community church which offers a wide range of activities, most of those involved in these activities will probably attend worship at Christmas and on some other festivals. Such a church might find that its normal Sunday attendance of 100 jumps to 500 at Christmas. In a small village of 250 people, with a normal attendance of 40, the Christmas carol service or the Harvest Festival might attract 150 – a very significant proportion of the total population. In other churches, particularly those which place a greater emphasis on the importance of committed membership, there might be almost no fringe in the sense described above. For most churches the fringe is likely to consist of the following groups of people:

- the parents of Sunday School children and Youth Group members;
- occasional worshippers;
- husbands, wives, and other family members of regular worshippers;

- people from outside the area visiting their families for the festival;
- people who have had recent contact with the church for weddings, baptisms, and funerals.

The main aim of the preacher on these occasions should be to present a central Christian truth in a way which refreshes established members, and interests those on the fringe. These festivals present a great opportunity for celebrating the core elements of the Christian gospel, and for offering some basic teaching on the incarnation, or the resurrection, or the gift of the Spirit. For most people attendance at church is only a part of the festival – a family gathering, a special meal, traditional television programmes, and weeks of secular preparation will all be involved. It is dangerous for the preacher to despise these elements. We cannot pretend that at Christmas the towns are not full of lights, hurrying frantic people, and carols pouring out of every department store loudspeaker. To ignore the Christmas dinner, the Queen's speech, and the opening of presents, is to give the message that we are not on the same wavelength as those who come to worship. We need somehow to acknowledge the joys and concerns which people bring, and to set them in the context of the Christian gospel as focused in the theme of the particular festival. This suggests that we should include the following elements in a "festival sermon":

- an acknowledgement of the celebration of the festival in the wider society;
- a basic telling of the gospel story;
- an explanation of the significance of the festival for the Christian faith;
- an exploration of the message of the festival for contemporary living.

FOLK FESTIVALS

In many places, the major "folk religion" festivals of Harvest and Mothering Sunday are now among the best attended occasions of the year, outstripping all except Christmas. Both are likely to have very large numbers of children present, and there may even be groups of Scouts, Guides, and other uniformed organizations "on parade". Most churches will have traditional rituals associated with these festivals – perhaps giving flowers to children on Mothering Sunday, or receiving gifts of produce at Harvest Festival.

The advantage of these occasions is that people come to church in a joyful frame of mind, expecting to thank God for his care expressed through creation or through family life. The difficulty is that these two festivals relate only obliquely to scripture or to the traditional Christian calendar. Recognizing that the expression of thanks to God is often the first step on the road to full Christian commitment may help us to address the needs of these congregations, and we may see these festivals as a way to lead people to explore more deeply the whole range of the Christian faith. The type of sermon which is appropriate will depend on the mixture of people in the congregation, and it is likely that a "family service" type of address will be most suitable.

NATIONAL OCCASIONS

The most obvious "national occasion" on which people attend church is Remembrance Day. Less regular events such as a significant anniversary of the monarch's succession are also celebrated in some churches, and may be attended by local politicians and dignitaries. There is a delicate balance which must be achieved by the preacher at these events. The risk is that they may become nothing more than eulogies of national pride, uncritically accepting the sentiments of those in the congregation.

The opposite risk, and just as great, is that some preachers spend so much effort attacking what is perceived to be the position of these groups that the groups are alienated from such preachers before they begin to say anything positive. These problems for the preacher are most likely to occur on Remembrance Sunday, when it can appear that the flags and processions of the British Legion are a glorification of war. Remembering and giving thanks for those who have died is a natural human emotion, and this is heightened when it occurs in the context of war. Many people are still genuinely grieving for sons or husbands killed in war; for them war is not something glorious. It is a great evil, and they remember it in part due to their determination that it should not happen again. This desire for peace can become a bridge between the congregation and the Christian gospel. A common recognition that the world and the nation both need saving from the effects of armed conflict immediately place both the preacher and the congregation on common ground, which can then be explored in the light of the gospel.

LOCAL EVENTS

In many communities the mayor and council attend church as a body for the "civic service". The preacher can see this as an opening to explore the nature of the local community in relation to the gospel, for there is at least an implicit recognition by the politicians that they are subject to divine authority. It should not, however, be treated as an invitation to lecture them on specific policies. Their desire to acknowledge their responsibilities in the context of worship should be positively valued. They should be prayed for, and should be encouraged in their tasks in the sermon. It is then possible to put before them the implications of the gospel for local government – perhaps by addressing the Christian understanding of the person and of society.

Similar questions arise when other local groups attend church corporately. A school might be celebrating a significant anniversary; the Women's Institute might be holding an annual service; local doctors and nurses might be attending a St Luke's service. These are not opportunities for the preacher to tell people what their function is – that would be presumptuous and offensive. The task of the preacher on such occasions is to be positive and supportive. These occasions are times when the distinctive Christian view of humanity and society can be explored, thus helping people to set their own contribution to the community in the wider context of God's purposes.

Exercise

Draw up a list of special occasions which occur in your own church. For each occasion write a brief description of the different groups of people likely to be present in the congregation.

15 PREACHING AT WEDDINGS AND FUNERALS

Among the largest congregations to gather at most churches are those which assemble for weddings and funerals. A funeral of a prominent person in the life of the town or village will certainly attract a church full of mourners, while the weddings of most young couples are attended by as many as two hundred guests. What is the value of preaching at these gatherings?

Some ministers prefer not to preach at weddings and funerals. They argue that the congregation's emotions are running so high that they are unable to concentrate on the sermon, and so will retain nothing of what is said. The address is seen only as an interruption to the main purpose of the service and, especially at a funeral, for most people only prolongs the embarrassment of an already difficult time.

Against this, we need to recognize that the family who come to the funeral or wedding have chosen to set this significant event in their lives in the context of Christian worship. We may have doubts about the depth of their commitment, and we may suspect that they are using the church as an attractive setting for their ceremony, or because there is no other generally accepted ritual for funerals in our society. It remains the case, however, that they are in a Christian setting, listening to the words of scripture and taking part in a Christian liturgy.

A wedding or a funeral is one of the most significant events in the lives of the people involved. At such times, people are raising, at least implicitly, a whole range of questions about the meaning of human life. At a wedding issues are being raised such as: the nature of the family; the creation of children; the nature of sexuality; the balance between the interests of the individual and society. At a funeral, people are naturally thinking of life and death, and will often openly be articulating questions about life after death.

All these concerns are natural openings for the Christian gospel; the preacher does not need to impose false questions on the congregation – those in the congregation are already asking these questions.

Gatherings of people at a wedding or funeral differ in one very important aspect from congregations on almost any other occasion – they have a clear common purpose and a shared reason for being present. This might be true to a lesser extent of the congregation at Christmas, or on Remembrance Sunday. It is much less true of the normal weekly congregation, for people attend church on a Sunday for a wide variety of different reasons. At a wedding or funeral there is a consensus among people about why they are there. Of course, they may well be bound together less by a desire to set this important life event in the context of the Church, than by a collection of traditional rituals which they feel must be carried out.

The correct way of mourning – black clothes, flowers, a wake after the service – all these are important. At a wedding the requirements of tradition are even more extensive. They include particular forms of dress, photographs, an elaborate reception, presents, and so on.

As a preacher you can take one of two attitudes to these traditions. Either you can work against them on the grounds that they are manifestations of folk religion which have nothing to do with the gospel, or you can try to build upon them, accepting that people are likely to be caught up in them whatever the preacher's attitude. It seems most sensible to recognize that these folk traditions surrounding marriage and death will continue whatever the preacher says. Indeed, most ministers accept that such rituals are a necessary way of expressing the important changes in the lives of individuals and the community which are taking place at such times. The minister who becomes positively involved in the celebration or the mourning is more likely to be listened to by those taking part. We need to explore ways of affirming these traditions and the people taking part in them, while using them as bases on which we can build in preaching.

In the chapter on "Preaching and culture" in Part One, I suggested that often the preacher will be addressing a particular sub-group in society. Frequently this will be the case in weddings and funerals. Even if the group at these services is not completely homogeneous, there is likely to be a narrower range of cultural sub-groups present than in most Sunday services. A funeral service might contain all the members of the local Rotary Club to which the deceased person belonged; the wedding might be celebrated for two travelling families; a doctor and a nurse might be marrying, and a high proportion of those present might belong to these professions. This suggests that you should not have a standard "wedding sermon" which is used on all such occasions, but should prepare something appropriate to say to these people, taking into account the language and assumptions of their sub-group. This will, of course, involve taking the time and the trouble to find out before the service what might be appropriate.

A question which exercises many people who preach at funerals is how much should be said about the deceased person, and in what terms. Some communities expect a full eulogy, extolling the virtues of the person who has died. There seems to be little, if any, merit in praising a person excessively, for it will inevitably sound hypocritical to those who knew the person well. On the other hand, it is natural to want to give thanks to God for the life someone has led, especially if their Christian example has inspired others. Giving thanks for a life, and committing the person to God's care, are natural emotions and should be expressed simply within the context of the Christian doctrine of resurrection.

Below is a list of general guidelines for preaching at weddings and funerals:

- the minister is there to serve people who have come to church for a specific purpose;
- this purpose should be set firmly in the context of the Christian gospel;
- a chief purpose of the worship and the sermon on these occasions is to help people to celebrate or to mourn;
- the sermon should set the event in the context of God's purposes for the individual and for the wider human community;
- the preacher should offer a view of a God who is loving and accepting – a God who shares in people's experiences of life and death.

Exercises

1. List the traditions and rituals which surround weddings and funerals in your church. How can these be built upon in preaching on these occasions?

2. Prepare an outline sermon for a wedding for two people you know based on one of the following readings:

   1 Corinthians 13, Ephesians 3.14–end, John 2.1–11.

3. Prepare an outline sermon for a funeral for someone you know who died recently based on one of the following readings:

   John 14.1–6, Romans 8.31–39, Revelation 21.1–7.

16 PREACHING AT ALL AGE WORSHIP

Adults and children are on a pilgrimage, journeying together. Neither adult nor child holds all the answers; each needs the other to progress along the path or the way. No longer can we allow the traditional family service to be a children's service, or a time when the church pays lip service to its children. At the most basic level, the organiser of the family service faces the challenge of occupying the adults' minds and, with luck, helping them to a more mature understanding of their faith, as well as satisfying the children's desire to worship with their whole person, body and mind. He or she must also seek to encourage adults to discover the child within them.[1]

Acts of all age worship, or "family services" as they are often called, have been one of the main growth areas in the churches in recent years. Many churches offer a monthly family service, and some have such worship weekly. Even in churches which do not describe their worship in such terms, there may well be services at which there is an age range of people from early childhood to retirement. In a congregation which contains such a mixture, especially when significant numbers of children are present, the structure and presentation of the sermon needs especially careful consideration.

Preparing a sermon for all age worship is not easier than a traditional sermon; if it is to be done well it is almost certainly more difficult. The model of one person standing at the front of the church and talking for fifteen minutes simply cannot be the standard form of address in all age worship. There is a variety of ways in which this pattern can be modified so as to involve more people.

- The preacher can conduct a conversation with the congregation, something which is easier to manage in churches with small congregations.

- The sermon can contain a question and answer session. Beware of difficult responses from the congregation, and be ready to deal with them.
- The sermon can be presented in dramatic form. This needs a considerable amount of preparation and rehearsal if it is to work successfully.
- A dialogue between two people can be an interesting way of presenting a sermon.
- One person could be interviewed by another person.
- Many churches are now equipped with overhead projectors – preparing slides which illustrate the address could add an extra dimension.
- Photographic slides may be used – for example slides of great works of art which can be bought at museums could be used in a sermon about the Cross.
- Some preachers have a gift for sketching. Illustrating while talking is difficult, but very effective.
- Glove puppets and ventriloquists' dummies can be effective – but do not use them every week.

Most of these methods can be used in "ordinary" preaching, but all need thorough preparation if they are to work. Do make sure that your "aids" really assist worship. Some preachers find a good idea or a good visual aid which they use at all costs whether or not it is a helpful illustration of what they are saying.

The danger which we must be aware of when preaching in all age acts of worship is that the content of the gospel is pitched at the level of the youngest child present, and is greatly over-simplified. We must find ways of expressing the simple but profound truths of the Christian gospel in such a way that it involves and interests all the people in the congregation, and at the same time does not under-value the challenge contained in scripture. This means that the language used must be as simple and direct as possible; you must use concrete images and vivid stories. It is particularly important to ensure that readings from the Bible are in a modern, easily understood translation.

Length is certainly important. Children, and many adults, cannot concentrate on one thing for a long time, especially when it consists of a lone person speaking. If the sermon can be integrated with other activities taking place in the service, this gives the preacher more time to develop a theme and ensures a higher level of interest among all members of the congregation.

Do not be afraid to address the great central doctrines of the Christian faith while preaching in all age worship. The preacher who shies away from addressing these things is not serving the congregation properly.

Exercises

1. Recall some good acts of all age worship which you have attended. Try to identify what made them particularly eoective.
2. Prepare a sermon for an act of all age worship in your church. If possible, you should involve a group of people in this preparation.

Notes

1. Sharon Swain, *The Sermon Slot*, Introduction.

Part Five

The History of Preaching

17 A BRIEF HISTORY OF PREACHING

However much the preacher tries to find his or her own style and to proclaim the gospel in contemporary idioms, each one still carries two thousand years of Christian preaching. This history cannot be dispensed with, and the preacher who knows and understands something of his or her antecedents will be the better for it. We are more free to be ourselves if we acknowledge the history which has shaped us.

The preaching tradition is strong. We may have moved out of the strait-jacket of the medieval *exemplum*, but there are equally strong conventions which operate on us – being aware of these unconscious constraints gives us the freedom to be innovative if we wish.

I am not aiming to give a detailed history on preaching in this chapter; merely to point to some of the main lines of development which have affected the way we now preach. The focus here is on the English sermon, primarily because the material is easily accessible, but also because it is this tradition which has affected the majority of preaching in the English-speaking countries.

Many sermons from the first centuries of the Church still exist. Some are long and allegorical, others brief and direct. In most of them a common pattern is visible: past prophecy leads to present divine events (particularly the resurrection of Jesus), and these issue a challenge to the hearers' present and future commitment, and behaviour.

John Stott's description of the preaching of John Chrysostom gives an indication of the quality of one of the most renowned preachers of the early Church:

> *Four chief characteristics of his preaching may be mentioned. First he was biblical. Not only did he preach systematically through several books, but his sermons are full of biblical quotations and allusions. Secondly, his interpretation of the scriptures was simple and straightforward. He followed the Antiochene school of "literal" exegesis, in contrast to fanciful Alexandrian allegorisations. Thirdly, his moral applications were down to earth. Reading his sermons today, one can imagine without*

difficulty the pomp of the imperial court, the luxuries of the aristocracy, the wild races of the hippodrome, in fact the whole life of an oriental city at the end of the fourth century. Fourthly, he was fearless in his condemnations. In fact, "he was a martyr of the pulpit, for it was chiefly his faithful preaching that caused his exile".[1]

PREACHING IN THE MEDIEVAL CHURCH

The history of the sermon as we know it began with the preaching friars, particularly the Franciscans and the Dominicans. They responded to a growing popular demand for sermons, and developed a technique which was to endure for centuries. From St Bernard of Siena (1380–1444) comes the following quotation, quite astonishing when one considers his dates: "If of these two things you can do only one – either hear the Mass or hear the sermon – you should let the Mass go rather than the sermon. There is less peril for your soul in not hearing Mass than in not hearing the sermon."

We possess a large number of medieval sermons, and this enables us to describe their structure and content. We must be aware, however, that most of those we have come from a very particular context – they were preached before the university as one of the exercises required for a master's degree. We have almost no examples. of ordinary sermons preached in parish churches to rustic congregations, and very few examples of the preaching of the friars in the market places. Having said that, the structure and style displayed in the formal sermon represented the teaching in sermon construction which the vast majority of clergy received, and so we can safely assume that it was the common pattern in England during the thirteenth and fourteenth centuries.

Thomas Waleys O.P., Master in Theology of the University of Oxford wrote *De modo componendi sermones cum documentis* in about 1340. It was to be the standard textbook on how to preach for about two hundred years. This book gives a clear scheme for preaching and it is worth looking at in detail.[2] Waleys describes the steps a preacher must follow in the sermon.

1. The first step is to announce the text which is to serve as the theme of the sermon. The text is the root from which the trunk and branches of the sermon will grow, and should contain within itself the whole sermon in germ. The text may be chosen from

anywhere in scripture, since it is all equally inspired, although some medieval writers prefer to restrict the choice of text to the Gospels, Epistles and Psalms. The text may not be modified, nor any words omitted from it which pervert the sense of the passage or leave it incomplete. For example, Waleys censures the preacher who, on the festival of St Thomas of Canterbury, took as his text 2 Kings 11.18 – "They slew the priest before the altar" – omitting the words "of Baal".

There are two pieces of advice on the choice of text. First, it should contain sufficient depth and quantity of meaning for development. Secondly, it should preferably contain three elements. Waleys gives as a good example Proverbs 11.8 "The *righteous* is *delivered* out of *trouble*." This three-fold rule was deeply ingrained in the preaching of the friars, and can be traced back as far as Augustine of Hippo. Augustine argued that the imprint of the Trinity can be discerned in the whole creation; all things possess a three-fold structure because they mirror their creator. It is, therefore, fitting that the sermon, the instrument of redemption, should also display this structure. Waleys adds that three points can be easily remembered and that a sermon with a three-fold structure cannot be over long. It is interesting that this structure persists into contemporary sermons, although most preachers who follow it do so unconsciously without being aware of the roots of the practice.

2. The text is followed by the ante-theme, the purpose of which is to introduce a bidding prayer. The ante-theme aims at capturing the imagination and goodwill of the listeners. It could be "by narrating some authentic marvel or prodigy of nature"; an example of how the devil is always working to impede the word of God; or by making clear to the hearers that the preacher is planning to win their souls not their money. The ante-theme should be very brief.

3. Next is the bidding prayer which should pick up one or more words of the text. So a sermon based on "prepare the way of the Lord" (notice the three-fold structure) could begin with the prayer "Let us prepare the way of the Lord, that he may come to us and instruct us."

4. After the prayer, the sermon itself begins with the introduction of the theme. It may start with a further quotation from scripture, or from a Christian or classical author. More generally this section

leads up to the statement of the theme as its conclusion. There are then two main ways of developing the theme – by narration or by argumentation. The use of "narration" includes extended analogies and stories from life. The "argumentation" mode follows a logical path by which the preacher leads to the theme. Smyth gives the following example: "Boys of noble birth, especially if prone to evil, are provided with a tutor of unblemished morals. Otherwise they would go to the bad. But we are of noble birth, being children of God, the King of all men, and the most excellent Queen, namely Holy Mother Church. Therefore we must be provided with the best of tutors. But the best of tutors is the Holy Spirit, to whom, among the divine persons, goodness is attributed by appropriation. Therefore it is fitting that we should have the Holy Spirit for our tutor. 'The Holy Ghost whom the Father will send in my name, he shall teach you.' (John 14.26)."

5. Then follows the division of the theme into three parts, corresponding to the three-fold structure of the chosen text. Alliteration and assonance often play an important part in this division, thus, for example, a sermon might have three parts headed "sorrow, salvation, and saintliness". Some medieval teachers of preaching recommended a much more complex rhetorical structure, including using three rhyming words for the division, and some even suggest keeping a personal list of rhyming words which can serve as the basis for sermons. Waleys is suspicious of "these rhetorical colours beloved by preachers of the modern generation, and sees no use in them except to tickle the ears of one's auditors" (Smyth, p. 29).
6. Finally, this structural skeleton is clothed with flesh. The ideas are developed, and the preacher appeals to the hearts and consciences of his hearers.

These rules of structure are followed in Waleys' book by advice on using the voice, gestures, length, and so on. For example, on the use of gestures he cautions dignity and restraint: "I have seen some preachers who seemed to be engaged in a sort of all in wrestling bout, hurling themselves about with such violence that they would have pushed the pulpit over if people had not rushed to hold it up."

Much of this medieval pattern seems to us to be false and contrived, and for many people calls into question the scope given to the Spirit in sermon preparation and delivery. The medieval sermon was not without its contemporary critics. Jacque de Lausanne writing in 1321 says, "Formerly when men preached in simple fashion they made numerous conversions, but later they came to preach in so pedantic a manner that the hearer, being no longer attentive to anything but the art of 'distinguishing' and 'dividing', carried away not the slightest spiritual or moral benefit from what was said to him."

There were, however, advantages to the medieval structure. It ensured that the preacher anchored the preparation firmly in the Bible, and the three-fold structure made sure that the hearer was given something manageable to remember. The problem was that, for many, the sermon was seen as merely a formal exercise. The text became a peg on which to hang an academic dissertation, and there was little compulsion to wrestle with the meaning of the gospel for contemporary society.

PREACHING AND THE REFORMATION

John Wycliffe (1329–84) was a forerunner of the Reformation. He complained about his contemporaries that "this ornamental style of preaching is little in keeping with God's word", and he affirmed that the sermon should expound the biblical passage, rather than single verse or short text. This appears to us to be straightforward advice, but not for a thousand years had this view been taken with such clarity. Wycliffe saw accurately that there are many dangers in isolating a single verse or phrase from scripture, and then trying to force it into an artificial structure. These dangers are generally avoided if a more substantial passage of the Bible – a whole parable, a chapter of an epistle, a complete psalm – became the basis for preaching. Wycliffe's evaluation of preaching was extremely high.

> *The highest service that men may attain to on earth is to preach the word of God. This service falls peculiarly to priests, and therefore God more straightly demands it of them. And for this cause, Jesus Christ left other works and occupied himself mostly in preaching, and thus did his apostles, and for this, God loved them. The Church, however, is honoured most by the preaching of God's word, and hence this the best service priests may render unto God.*

The greatest achievement of the Reformation was to reinstate scripture to its rightful place, at the centre of the Christian life and of the Church. The high place given to scripture, together with the equally important event of the invention of printing, meant that lay people became eager to have the Bible expounded, and that for the first time both clergy and laity had relatively easy access to scripture.

E.C. Dargen's comment succinctly describes the importance of the events of the sixteenth century:

> *The great events and achievements of that mighty revolution [the Reformation] were largely the work of preachers and preaching; for it was by the word of God, through the ministry of earnest men who believed, loved and taught it, that the best and most enduring work of the Reformation was done. And conversely, the events and principles of the movement powerfully reacted on preaching itself, giving it a new spirit, new power, new forms, so that the relation between the Reformation and preaching may be succinctly described as one of mutual dependence, aid and guidance.*

In Britain the effect of the reformers on the sermon was seen most clearly in the work of the seventeenth-century Puritans. Many of them were unlearned, humble people, who expounded the Bible in their own idiom.

The Puritan preaching tradition influenced the Church of England, especially through John Tillotson (1630–94). This archbishop of Canterbury was an heir to the Puritans, and stressed simplicity of life and a natural uncontrived method of expression in preaching. He complained that often the general sense of the text was neglected, while each word was separately considered in all its possible meanings. He insisted that the preacher should appeal to reason and to common sense, and he placed an emphasis on the moral consequences of a faithful response to scripture. Above all, he preached that reasonableness, in belief and behaviour, were essential marks of Christianity.

> *Now religion doth purify our minds and refine our spirits by quenching the fire of lust and suppressing the fumes and vapours of it, and by scattering the clouds and mists of passion. And the more any man's soul is cleansed from the filth and dregs of sensual lusts the more nimble and expedite it will be in its operation. The more any man conquers his passions, the more calm and sedate his spirit is, and the geater equality he maintains in his temper, his*

> *apprehensions of things will be the more clear and unprejudiced, and his judgement more firm and steady. And this is the meaning of that saying of Solomon, he that is slow to wrath is of great understanding, but he that is hasty of spirit exalteth folly.*

So strong was the influence of Tillotson that for the next hundred years his sermons were continually in print. Not only did they serve as a model for Anglican preaching, but many generations of clergy would read Tillotson's sermons from the pulpit.

John Wesley (1703–91) and George Whitefield (1714–70) signalled the beginning of what is generally regarded as the high point of English preaching – the period from about 1750 until the end of the nineteenth century. Above all, Wesley and Whitefield were missionary preachers; the great bulk of their work was directed at those outside the church structures. In their preaching we find a direct, personal challenge and invitation. Their sermons appeal to the emotions and to the depths of religious feeling. Wesley himself had an experience in which he felt his heart "strangely warmed", and in which he had been assured of the forgiveness of his sins. His sermons proclaimed the message of free salvation which he himself had received. To his contemporaries raised on the objective, general, and impersonal preaching of the Hanoverian Church, Wesley sounded almost offensively personal in the way he addressed his sermons to individuals. So effective was he, that people gathered in their thousands to hear him, and grown working men wept openly as they were moved by his words.

> *My message is to thee, sinner! I stand here today to bring thee to bethink thyself of thy past ways. Thou who dost now appear in the presence of thy God – loathsome in thy sins – I challenge and command thee to bow thy stubborn neck, and to bend thy knee. Dost not thou, even thou ungrateful as thy hast been these many years – yea a hardened rebel from thy mother's breast until now – dost thou not hear the Saviour calling to thee, to repent and turn? Was it not for thee that he shed his blood? Did he not carry thy sorrows to Calvary, even thine? Was he not wounded for thy transgressions? Did he not think of thee, of thy soul, and of all its abominations that dark night when he lay in agony on the ground? Yes. It was none other than thy sins that made his sweat blood in that garden. But now, with a purpose of mercy in his heart toward thy wretched soul he calls thee to himself.*

Whitefield, although less well known in our age was, perhaps, an even greater preacher than Wesley. He saw the task of preaching as the highest form of Christian service and, equally important, he insisted that listening to the sermon was an essential Christian duty.

> *In Britain and America (which he visited 7 times), indoors and out of doors, he averaged about twenty sermons a week for 34 years. Eloquent, zealous, dogmatic, passionate, he enlivened his preaching with vivid metaphors, homely illustrations and dramatic gestures. By these he would hold his audiences spellbound, as he either addressed direct questions to them or begged them earnestly to be reconciled with God. He had complete confidence in the authority of his message, and was determined that it should receive the respect it deserved as God's word. Once in a New Jersey meeting house he "noticed an old man settling down for his accustomed, sermon time nap" writes John Pollack, one of his biographers. Whitefield began his sermon quietly without disturbing the gentleman's slumbers. But then in measured, deliberate words he said: "If I had come to speak to you in my own name, you might rest your elbows upon your knees and your heads on your hands and go to sleep! But I have come to you in the name of the Lord God of Hosts and (he clapped his hands and stamped his foot) I must and I will be heard." The old man woke up startled.*[3]

Charles Simeon (1759–1838), vicar of Holy Trinity Church Cambridge, devoted his attention to the techniques of preaching for 40 years. Generations of evangelical undergraduates attended the classes in sermon composition which he gave in his rooms in King's College. When he died he left behind him 21 volumes of sermon outlines, but he is better remembered for the many pieces of advice which he gave to his pupils. Simeon revived the notion that it is possible to teach people to preach, and that such teaching is an essential part of preparation for the ministry. Many of his best sayings survived in the writings of his pupils.

> *Be most solicitous to ascertain from the original and from the context the true, faithful and primary meaning of every text.*

> *Do not preach what you can tell, but what your people can receive. Suppose I have six narrow mouthed glass bottles to fill. I have both a large pail brim full of water, and a small*

> *tea kettle with a tapered spout also full of water. Which of the two shall I use in filling the narrow mouthed bottles?*
>
> *Let your preaching come from the heart. Love should be the spring of all actions, and especially of a minister's. If a man's heart be full of love, he will rarely offend. He may have severe things to say, but he will say them in love. People soon see whether a minister is speaking in his own spirit, or merely declaring God's message.*
>
> *Beware of laying emphasis on every word, or with great frequency. Rather mark importance by management of time than of stress, except in special cases. Just as it is in music. Group a sentence together by rapid enunciation, and mark the emphasis by pauses between the more emphatic parts.*

The following piece of advice is, perhaps, of especial relevance to many people within the church today. Simeon was very cautious of extemporary preaching, both for himself and for others.

> *I do not advise any young minister to preach extempore until he has preached three or four hundred written sermons; until he has been at least three or four years preaching. Let him speak meanwhile, extempore in his workhouse or schoolroom addresses, the same sermon which he has delivered in Church from writing. He will thus acquire the habit of speaking easily and efficiently. After a few years, let him drop the fully written sermon and copious notes, and then gradually pass to extempore speaking. Carefully let him avoid anything like slovenly preparation. Let his extempore preaching be neither the result nor the cause of indolence. To begin extempore preaching too soon is likely to lead to crudeness of style. Never forget that you have to win souls. It takes more time to prepare properly for an extempore sermon than to write one. There are but few good extempore preachers in England, partly because men do not devote sufficient time and effort to preparation. Evangelical preachers too often take routine texts, which they may easily prate about, but comparatively seldom choose texts which require study and thinking over.*[4]

Books of sermons were published in vast numbers from the middle of the nineteenth century until well into the twentieth century. Most of them make very dull reading, and although they are of interest to a student of the history of preaching, few of them are of real use to the contemporary preacher. They do, however, have something to tell us about the difference between the written text and the preached sermon. To us the words on the page may seem dull and lifeless; yet there are countless stories about people flocking in their thousands to hear them and being deeply moved by these words.

The usual consensus is that preaching has declined during the twentieth century. Perhaps the main cause of this has been a decline in the power of the spoken word generally. Some notable figures have worked hard to reinstate the task of preaching to its rightful place. The most prominent among these in England have been Martin Lloyd-Jones who was minister of Westminster Chapel in London from 1938–68, and Donald Coggan, Archbishop of Canterbury from 1974–80.

What has this brief look at the history of preaching taught us? First, that there have been frequent "rediscoveries" of the importance of preaching. Many times the sermon has fallen into a subordinate position. Often it has become dry and formalized, and indeed for long periods sermons have simply not been preached. We have seen, however, that at significant points in Christian history the office of the preacher has received renewed attention, and the centrality of the sermon in the Christian community has been reassessed and given its rightful place.

Secondly, each generation in which preaching has been renewed has seen structure and technique as important. Tillotson, Simeon, Lloyd-Jones, and many others have all held that good sermon structure and technique do not hinder the word of God from breaking through, but are, on the contrary, necessary. Structure enables listeners to hear and appropriate the message. The danger is that structure degenerates into formalism; that structure itself becomes the aim of the exercise, and the gospel message takes second place. We must be reminded that good structure and technique are necessary, and are indeed the work of the Spirit; but we must also be aware that they are tools to use and not ends in themselves.

Thirdly, each generation needs to develop its own authentic preaching style. Medieval or Victorian sermons sound strange to our ears, and it is too easy to dismiss them as chained by conventions or by the assumptions of their age. Our preaching is limited in the same way, but despite these limitations we can still find a distinctive style which speaks to our listeners.

This brief survey of preaching in the past has shown that it is possible to gain an objective view of our preaching by looking at the sermon in different historical periods. It is a useful exercise for you as a student of preaching to take some time reading sermons from the past, and noting their structure and content, and to ask how this sheds light on your own understanding of the contemporary task of preaching.[5]

Exercises

1. Do you recognize any of the descriptions of preaching in the past in the sermons of your own church?
2. Does a study of the history of preaching have anything useful to teach us about preaching in the present?

Notes

1. From John Stott, *I Believe in Preaching*, p. 21, describing John Chrysostom.
2. This description is abbreviated from Charles Smyth, *The Art of Preaching*, pp. 20–41.
3. John Stott, *I Believe in Preaching*, pp. 32–33.
4. Quotations taken from Charles Smyth, *The Art of Preaching*, pp. 176–8.
5. For more detailed introductions to the history of preaching the following are especially interesting:
   John Stott, *I Believe in Preaching*, Hodder & Stoughton, 1982, ch. 1;
   Charles Smyth, *The Art of Preaching: A Practical Survey of Preaching in the Church of England 747–1939*, SPCK, 1940;
   The English Sermon (3 Volumes), eds Martin Seymour-Smith, C.H. Sisson and Robert Nye, Carcanet Press, 1976.
   Paul A. Welsby, *Sermons and Society*, Pelican, 1970.

BIBLIOGRAPHY

This is not intended to be an extensive bibliography of books on preaching. It does contain all the books referred to or used in the text, and also covers most of the main areas discussed.

Adams, Jay, *A Consumer's Guide to Preaching*, Victor Books, 1991.

Allen, Ronald, *Preaching the Topical Sermon*, Westminster Press, 1992.

Berry, Cicily, *Your Voice and how to use it Successfully*, Virgin, 1990.

Board of Mission of the General Synod, *Good News in Our Times*, Church House Publishing, 1991.

Browne, R. E. C., *The Ministry of the Word*, SCM Press, 1958.

Buttrick, David, *Homiletic*, SCM Press, 1987.

Clark, Neville, *Preaching in Context*, Kevin Mayhew, 1991.

Cleverly Ford, D. W., *New Preaching from the Old Testament*, Mowbrays, 1976.

Coggan, Donald, *The Sacrament of the Word*, Fount, 1987.

Dennis, Trevor, *Speaking of God*, Triangle, 1992.

Division of Ministries of the Methodist Church, *Faith and Worship: Local Preachers Training Course*, Methodist Publishing House, 1990.

Fuller, Reginald, *The Use of the Bible in Preaching*, Bible Reading Fellowship, 1981.

Gilmore, Alec, *Tomorrow's Pulpit*, Lutterworth Press, 1975.

Gowan, Donald, *Reclaiming the Old Testament for the Christian Pulpit*, T. & T. Clark, 1980.

Henderson, J. Frank, *Preparing to Preach*, Novalis, Ottowa, 1991.

Hook, Dan, *Effective Preaching*, E.J. Dwyer, 1991.

Hull, John, *What Prevents Christian Adults from Learning?*, SCM Press, 1984.

Hunter, A. M., *Preaching the New Testament*, SCM Press, 1981.

Hybels, B., Briscoe, S., Robinson, H., *Mastering Contemporary Preaching*, Inter-Varsity Press, 1991.

Ireson, Gordon, *A Handbook of Parish Preaching*, Mowbray, 1982.

Jones, Richard, *Groundwork of Worship and Preaching*, Epworth Press, 1980.

Killinger, John, *Fundamentals of Preaching*, SCM Press, 1985.

Kooienga, William, *Elements of Style for Preaching*, Zondervan, 1989.

Lloyd-Jones, D. Martin, *Preaching and Preachers*, Hodder & Stoughton, 1971.

Mitchell, Henry, *The Recovery of Preaching*, Hodder & Stoughton, 1977.

Newbigin, Lesslie, *Foolishness to the Greeks*, SPCK, 1986.

Noren, Carol, *The Woman in the Pulpit*, Abingdon Press, 1991.

Nye, Robert, Seymour-Smith, Martin, Sission C.H. (eds), *The English Sermon 1550–1850* (3 vols), Carcanet Press, 1976.

Outler, Albert, *John Wesley's Sermons: An Introduction*, Abingdon Press, 1991.

Sachs, Jonathan, *The Persistence of Faith*, Weidenfeld & Nicolson, 1991.

Sangster, William, *The Craft of Sermon Illustration*, Epworth Press, 1954.

Shearlock, David, *The Practice of Preaching*, Churchman Publishing, 1990.

Smyth, Charles, *The Art of Preaching, 747–1939*, SPCK, 1940.

Stacey, John, *Preaching Reassessed*, Epworth Press, 1980.

Stewart, James, *Preaching*, English Universities Press, 1955.

Stott, John, *I Believe in Preaching*, Hodder & Stoughton, 1982.

Swain, Sharon, *The Sermon Slot* (2 vols), SPCK, 1992, 1993.

Theissen, Gerd, *Sign Language of Faith: Opportunities for Preaching Today*, SCM Press, 1995.

Wagley, Lawrence, *Preaching with the Small Congregation*, Abingdon Press, 1989.

Welsby, Paul, *Sermons and Society*, Penguin, 1970.

Williams, Howard, *My Word*, SCM Press, 1973.

Wilson, Paul, *A Concise History of Preaching*, Abingdon Press, 1992.